Praise for ***The Ten***

"Ilyse has written a slim volume with a lot of heart—a beautiful introduction to the actual *doing* of IFS therapy. This book will help people who are new to IFS to try it on, like a new pair of glasses, but these glasses are for looking inward. The author weaves her own parts stories into the pages, making the journey feel friendly and accessible to anyone. Thank you, Ilyse. Your work will inspire many to heal their traumatized parts with IFS therapy."

—**Colleen West**, LMFT, IFS approved consultant and author of *We All Have Parts*

"*The Tender Parts* is a key source of support and guidance for anyone who is looking to heal themselves. Ilyse Kennedy's personal stories make the teachings of IFS come to life. She provides thoughtful reflections in each section to help deepen our understanding of ourselves so that we can explore and heal our own parts."

—**Tracy Dalgleish**, PhD, C.Psych., psychologist, writer, and relationship expert

"*The Tender Parts* is both poetic and practical. This gem of a book combines clear, step-by-step instructions on how to access the IFS model with the depth and poignancy of the writer's own inner world. It is an important contribution to the literature on IFS therapy."

—**Lisa Spiegel**, MA, LMHC, author of *Internal Family Systems Therapy with Children*

"*The Tender Parts* is a beautiful synopsis of IFS and how it can be applied, practically and clinically, to working with our inner worlds. Ilyse does a fantastic job of sharing her own tender parts, her clinical expertise, and her creative exercises that allow the reader to fully grasp IFS and all it has to offer."

—**Justin Martin**, MA, LMHC, @partsofmetherapy

"In *The Tender Parts*, Ilyse Kennedy has gone far beyond an articulation of healing theory, which she does thoughtfully and beautifully. She offers herself as a vulnerable guidepost for understanding what it means to truly welcome and witness internalized parts. Seamlessly shifting between explanation, examples, and expressive exercises, Kennedy allows for the reader to integrate as they move through the material. This is a wonderfully conceptualized book, and complex concepts are digested with ease as the book unfolds with gentleness and grace."

—Sana Powell, LPC

"Engaging, informative, and refreshingly honest. Ilyse Kennedy blends her lived experience and clinical knowledge beautifully to guide readers into the IFS model and into befriending their own internal systems. I can't wait to recommend this book to clients and clinicians alike!"

—Tyndal E. Schreiner, MA, LPC

"Ilyse's acceptance of her own parts creates space for the raw, forsaken, tender parts of others. Upon accepting the book's invitation—some might say challenge—the reader is expertly guided through transformative steps toward one's Self. A must-read."

—Lindsay Camp, LMFT

"Ilyse does a beautiful job inviting you to explore all of your parts with curiosity, compassion, and nonjudgment, reminding you that no matter what, you are already whole. This is the first book every trauma survivor should read to understand their internal experience."

—Yolanda Renteria, LPC, somatic experiencing coach

"*The Tender Parts* is for all of us. Whether you're a clinician holding space for the wounded or a human facing your own wounds for the first (or tenth) time, this book will help you bravely step into the lifelong work of feeling at home in your own body. Your inner world is waiting."

—Alexis Edwards, LCSW-S, certified BEST Doula, founder Birth 360

THE TENDER PARTS

A Guide to Healing from Trauma through Internal Family Systems Therapy

Ilyse Kennedy, LPC, LMFT, PMH-C

Published by
PESI Publishing, Inc.
3839 White Ave
Eau Claire, WI 54703

Cover: Emily Dyer
Editing: Jenessa Jackson, PhD
Layout: Emily Dyer and Alissa Schneider

ISBN: 9781683735540 (print)
ISBN: 9781683735557 (ePUB)
ISBN: 9781683735564 (ePDF)

Printed in the United States of America.

About the Author

Ilyse Kennedy, LPC, LMFT, PMH-C, is a trauma therapist who owns Moving Parts Psychotherapy, a group practice in Austin, TX. Like many practitioners, she entered this field after many years on the couch and plenty of time healing from her own trauma. As a therapist, she works with clients of all ages, most of whom are recovering from complex trauma. After recognizing the need for wider education and support regarding trauma, she began advocacy work on Instagram to offer further information around trauma and its impact, with the goal of normalizing the experience for trauma survivors and creating more understanding among the general public. She has also shared her work at various conferences and organizations, and she hosts a monthly consultation and education group with clinicians around the world. Having considered herself a writer since she could first craft stories, Kennedy looks forward to expanding her advocacy work into book form as well. While she is proud of her accolades in the mental health field, she is proudest of her children, who show the benefits of presence and playfulness each and every day.

Dedication

For my clients who have graciously allowed me to meet and be with their most tender parts, this book is for you.

Table of Contents

Acknowledgments

Writing a book while running a full-time group therapy practice during pregnancy could not have happened without the beautiful support network who nourished me, sustained me, and gave me endless encouragement.

First, I thank my husband and partner, Brandon, who assured time and emotional energy for me to write, putting his own obligations to the side so I could make this dream come true. He knew I could do this when I wasn't so sure. To my children, Camilla, Levi, and Maxine, who helped form the parts of me I needed to access to become the mother, therapist, and author who wrote this book. I learned to delight in myself through the delight I find so effortlessly in you. Thank you for offering your pride, for our precious time together, and for being the reason behind my healing before I could do it for myself.

Endless gratitude to my parents, Faith and Bernard, who always believed I would do big, wonderful things, even when I didn't. And to my sister, Jenna, who cheered me on from afar. Thanks to my late grandparents, Lois and Mickey, whose energy I felt guiding me through this process. Though I was never able to share the exciting news of my first book, I could feel your presence and encouragement as I wrote. If Mickey could write his first book in his nineties, I could do it in my thirties.

To the clients who have shared their sacred stories and have given me the honor of being a part of their healing process, this book is yours as much as it is mine. You have taught me more about being a therapist and human than I ever could have learned in graduate school. I cherish the ways we show up for each other. Thank you for your continued trust in me.

To my therapist, Ann, who makes space for my parts each week in whatever way they need to show up and who gently held my fearful parts throughout the writing process.

To the mentors who honed my therapist parts until Self-energy was able to flow through me: Brianne Blevins, Sunny Lansdale, and Marshall Lyles.

To the women in my group texts, who validated my immense undertaking and never shamed me when I could still update them on the latest goings-on of *The Real Housewives*: Alyssa and Lindsay, and Alexis, Lacey, and Lexi. And to my therapist colleague, Samantha Montemayor: Our ability to nerd out and laugh at our profession (and ourselves) at the same time is something I cherish.

Thank you to my IFS home group: Jen, Trish, David, and Traci, who met my parts alongside me. In the safe communal space we've created I'm able to find my Self-energy, accessing healing, laughter, and an endless affinity for you all.

Thank you to the Moving Parts Psychotherapy Instagram community, who found something special in my voice. You gave me the platform to write this in-depth work. In it, I hope you find the extension of what you seek from my posts.

Most importantly, I thank the PESI Publishing team. Thank you to Karsyn for believing my work could translate to book form and knowing there was an audience for it. Thank you to Jenessa for your beautiful, supportive editing that honed this book into the work it was meant to be. And to Kayla, who saw this book through to the end.

Finally, thank you to the reader. I hope you find what you are looking for within these pages. It is with great honor that I write for you and the tender parts that show up alongside as you navigate these pages.

Introduction

At age 22, I was surprised to find myself sitting on a turquoise couch in a therapist's office in Los Angeles. I say that with surprise because I can't recall what finally made me book the appointment. Perhaps it was the recognition that existing felt excruciating, but I didn't know any different. Perhaps it was the tumultuous relationship I was in. Perhaps it was the terror I experienced each time I left the house. I had driven by the sign for that therapy office each day on the way home from a job that I often left exhausted and in tears. The sign for the office was easy to spot, just above a wine bar on Sunset Boulevard. As I sat across from my new therapist, Sarah, my story came flooding out of me.

After I finished speaking, Sarah looked at me tenderheartedly and said, "Of course you've been having a hard time. You experienced immense trauma."

For a long time, I had become the bad things that happened to me. But when Sarah termed my experience as trauma, I felt like I could finally take ownership over the reality that these bad things had happened *to* me.

While it changed the course of my healing to take this ownership, the acknowledgment and realization alone wasn't enough to change my day-to-day struggles. Following the initial recognition of trauma, Sarah took the treatment on from all angles. She recommended some books that I might find useful, but I did little more than press "buy now" on Amazon. My anxiety wouldn't allow me the space to look inside. She also suggested diagnoses such as depression, anxiety, and posttraumatic stress disorder (PTSD) but didn't help me understand what they meant. She countered my self-deprecating and shaming thoughts with positive reframes, but I wasn't able to take them in. Despite the extent of treatment options provided, nothing Sarah tried seemed to truly affect me. I felt her hopelessness in my treatment, that even she didn't know how to help me. Although I desperately wanted to be *better*, I didn't know how *better* would happen for me, or even what it would feel like.

Ten years later, I am now sitting in the therapist's chair rather than on a turquoise couch. In my work as a therapist, I aim to offer clients an understanding of trauma *and* help them resolve their trauma through deepening their understanding of themselves. That's because in a culture saturated with toxic positivity, we get messages that make real and lasting change seem as easy as "choose joy" or "let go." I felt this in my interactions with Sarah. This desire to be positive is well-intentioned, but it negates everything that makes up our personhood. It disavows our cultural background, the relationships that have shaped us, and the traumas we have endured.

Instead of holding the belief that humans are simplistic creatures who can shift their mood or perspective on a dime, what if we consider the complexities of our internal makeup? What if we recognize that we are not a single thing but, instead, made of many internal parts who, with each facet of life we have endured, have learned to do different jobs in order to keep us safe and fully functioning?

Internal family systems therapy (IFS), developed by Richard C. Schwartz, does just that. IFS maintains that we are born with a core "Self" but that in response to each event we endure, our system becomes fragmented and we form a variety of parts within us that aid in our functioning. If we look deeply enough, we can get to know these parts. Just as IFS introduces the idea of parts, it also maintains that we all have access to wholeness in the form of "Self-energy"—a feeling of being centered, like an energy well that offers parts access to compassion, understanding, and trust. By expanding Self-energy, we expand our capacity to understand, and rationally respond to, what is happening inside ourselves and others.

When I first heard about the concept of IFS in my graduate studies, I felt so much relief. I felt this not just for future clients whom I would have the privilege of sharing this framework for trauma recovery, but also for myself. I had spent so much time trying to change my thought patterns with little success. So much time perceiving myself in black and white. When I considered, instead, that I held various parts within me—parts that had formed in response to the things that happened to me—I could hold compassion and make more space for all of me. My own journey of getting to know my parts began that day. As you get to know your own parts through the pages of this book, I will join you on this journey by introducing you to mine.

> *There is a vacationing part of me floating on the ocean in Cape Cod. She shows up in whispers, usually when I see no blank spaces in my schedule. She sips a margarita, there in the middle of the ocean, as if Jimmy Buffet himself placed it in her saltwater-pruned hands, letting me know I need a vacation.*
>
> *There is a people-pleasing part of me who can't say no. She shows up as soon as anyone makes a request of me. "Of course," she says, before a conscious thought steps in to say, "You don't have the mental capacity to do that right now."*

There is a part of me stuck beneath a Mickey Mouse blanket on her parents' couch. She is 17 and frozen. She worries if she lifts the blanket, her body will, once again, no longer be her own.

There is a part of me who is 22. I can feel a churning in my stomach and a sinking sensation in the center of my chest that lets me know she's awakened. She holds the word trauma *tightly in her hands and on her heart. The word feels like her permission—allowing her to acknowledge the weight of her experience—and sometimes her shield, protecting her from the burdens of the outside world. She stands on the edge of a black hole. She walks closer to it, peering over the edge. Another part comes in to block her before she gets too close.*

Perhaps, inside you, there also lives a carefree tourist reminding you to pause before you burn out. Perhaps there is a people pleaser, afraid to say no for fear that you'll be hurt once again. Perhaps there is a teenager, perpetually stuck in the trauma they endured. And maybe, there is a part who holds the label "trauma victim" firmly in their hands and the statement "I am bad" tightly around their heart.

Whatever the reason this book has found itself in your hands, I want you to know, dear reader, that this book is a journey. In the therapy room, it is my goal to ensure clients feel my presence with them. While we are not physically together, I want you to know that I am accompanying you in what lies ahead. You will get to know my voice and my presence. Think of me as your caring other. If the work or concepts in these pages begin to feel too big or too much, it is okay to put the book down. It is okay to return to it later or to forgo the book altogether. Throughout this book, I will offer you periodic reminders and space to check in with yourself and your system.

WHOM THIS BOOK IS FOR

This book is for 22-year-old me, who tried over and over again to write her trauma narrative while she was still stuck in it. Who was given the word *trauma* with little direction of how to heal it. This book is for other survivors who hold the same word close but don't know where to go from there. This book is for those looking for a framework to support and understand a loved one who is a trauma survivor. This book is for clinicians—the sacred story keepers—seeking to understand and aid trauma survivors from an affirming and sensitive lens. This book is for those holding the sacred stories of others, in addition to their own. Through this book, you will understand more about trauma through an IFS lens and get to know the makeup of your own system through information, exercises, and reflections.

As you begin this work, I offer you my full Self-energy. As I write these words, I feel it ignite in the center of my chest, a glow illuminating around my heart. The 22-year-old is tucked away in her bed, and I have planned to check in with her later. The 17-year-old is safe in her room, being serenaded by Justin Timberlake through a set of headphones. The people pleaser has made it clear (and asked me to let you know) that she hopes you enjoy this book, but she'll be relaxing with the vacationing part in Cape Cod, holding a cold margarita, but not taking a sip. With my parts to the side and my Self-energy illuminating from my heart to yours, we begin.

1

Am I Not Whole?

There is a part of me who struggles with beginnings. Who couldn't get the first sentence of this book down on paper. I feel frustration toward this part of me. It first showed up as a pull in my chest that stopped my breath. The pull turned soon to a sensation of stuckness.

When I close my eyes and check in with this part, it feels familiar. I ask it if there is anything it wants me to know. It shows me an image of my high school history teacher smiling—a teacher so beloved by students but who didn't care for me. The image becomes clearer as I focus on the stuck sensation and image at the same time. I see 15-year-old me reflected back in his glasses. I feel shame rise from this part and from this younger version of myself. I feel her with us now, though the initial part is protecting her. The sensation of stuckness sinks into my stomach, as if quicksand is slowly pulling this part and this younger me down.

As I notice the shame and the viscous sensation of the dragging sand, I begin to feel differently toward this part. It's as if compassion is breaking through, like sunlight coming through the clouds. I ask the part, "How would you feel about not having to do your job anymore?" The stuckness firms and I feel an answer come to me. "I'm afraid we would fail," the part replies. I begin to feel sadness toward this part. I check in with it to see if it can feel my presence. It can. I let it know I'm feeling sad toward it. It's able to take in the sadness without taking it on. The stuckness in my chest loosens as the part comes closer to me. I let it know, "I understand you're protecting the young one." It feels understood and comes closer.

As humans, we are born whole. Our nervous systems are perfectly built to receive connection and safety from those around us. We come into the world seeking an experience of safety and believe those around us will provide that by meeting our needs—until we learn otherwise. With each need met as an infant—a cry that is comforted by the warmth of a loving other, one that is met with milk, and another that is soothed with a gentle rock to sleep—our safety is affirmed. However, when enough of our needs are not met, we begin to develop adaptations either to get our needs met or to suppress them. Even with our extremely limited experience of the world at this age, our tiny nervous systems begin to internalize and differentiate what keeps us safe from what causes danger. Perhaps we learn to smile and coo to get our caregivers to engage because they don't respond to our cries. Or maybe our caregivers are unpredictable in their response to us, so we approach them with hesitation, not knowing whether to allow ourselves to take in safety or put up a wall to block unpredictability. In some cases, we may learn to suppress our own needs, such as dimming hunger and bathroom cues, because we come to expect that these needs won't be met.

As we take in information and learn about the world from these relational and environmental cues, our brains begin to form patterns of relating that become known as our "states of mind" (Siegel, 2012). Our earliest brain states form in response to the experiences we have with our caregivers, but they dictate how we interact with the world going forward, even into adulthood. In other words, we learn how to interact based on the ways our needs were met (or not met) and how our interactions were received. In IFS, these brain states reflect the adaptations that we call parts.

These parts feel like entities within us, each holding their own emotions, sensations, memories, behaviors, roles, or jobs. With each new tribulation we endure, these parts form within us to help us cope and better respond to similar situations in the future. These parts take on different jobs within our system and carry burdens in response to the hardships we have experienced. For example, we might develop a people-pleasing part in response to our needs not being met in infancy. We might develop a depressed part who helps to numb our emotions. Or we might develop a rage part who believes it is protecting us from being hurt.

These parts each serve a purpose, so no part is considered "good" or "bad" (Schwartz, 2021). However, our tendency is to look away from the parts of us that we believe are bad, wrong, or unhelpful in some way. Many of us hold the belief that if we look away from something, it keeps it at bay. But what we actually find is if we ignore our parts, they try harder to be heard and come on stronger. In contrast, when we pause and get to know them, they tend to soften and feel more in control. As you learn more about IFS in this book, you'll get to know your own parts.

If this concept of parts is still hard to envision right now, think of the Pixar movie *Inside Out*. In this movie, a young girl named Riley navigates the stressors of starting at a new middle school after she moves across the country with her family. Rather than making Riley the focus of the movie, we meet her emotions, who are aptly named Joy, Sadness, Anger, Disgust, and Fear (Docter, 2015). In the movie, these emotions appear as physical entities, and they function as characters with their own roles, emotions, beliefs, and interactions with others. This is often how parts show up too.

As with *Inside Out*, the multiplicity of parts within us can represent different emotions, adaptations, body sensations, past versions of ourselves, roles, or facets of our personality. In addition, parts can reflect the concept of "internalized others," in which the parts that live within us represent people from the outside world whom we have internalized, rather than as adaptations (Badenoch, 2008). These outside people can reflect others who have been loving to us or people who have hurt us. Daniel Siegel (2012) calls this concept "MWe"—the internalizing of "Me + We"—in relation to states of mind. When we internalize others who aid us in organizing our internal world, it helps us form coherent states of mind. But when we internalize others who feel chaotic or disorganized, it leads our states of mind into a place of chaos, and we develop even more parts to help us organize back to a place of coherence.

If this is your first time learning about IFS, the concept of parts may feel foreign to you because it does not represent the way you think about the human experience or your own internal experience. With time, it may feel more comforting and settle in your own system with ease.

♡ Reflection

I invite you to take a moment to pause. Notice your breath. Are any sensations arising in your body? How is the concept of parts sitting with you so far? Does it feel welcoming or foreign? Does it feel relieving to take in, or do you notice some resistance? Do you feel yourself orienting to the idea or is confusion arising? If you notice resistance or confusion, this is okay! Acknowledge where it is showing up in or around your body. Is there anything it might need from you in order to ease?

As a trauma survivor, learning about IFS felt like a huge relief for my own system. My trauma brain had adapted to think in black and white—as if I was either in danger or safe. My internal alarm was sounding off and launching me into a trauma response, or I was completely at rest (a part of me might even call that version "lazy"). It felt like I was constantly lingering somewhere between anxiety and depression, the bookends of my threat responses. My life felt chaotic, with no reprieve, and those around me also felt my chaos. Between the parts of me that were numbed with alcohol at night and the parts that felt terrified during the day, I clung to my partner for a sense of stability and calm that my own system struggled to provide me with. At that time, I didn't have the language of parts. I would think to myself, "I am chaotic." But when I found the language and began to adjust how I spoke about myself and to myself, I became softer and more compassionate toward my parts. When I shifted to using IFS language, "I am chaotic" transformed into "A part of me is chaotic" or even "The 22-year-old has a part that is chaotic."

Making this simple shift in language represents a huge change from traditional psychotherapy approaches that seek to find the "problem" and determine a solution or treatment path. Within IFS, instead of viewing behaviors and symptoms as "disorders," we view different parts of ourselves as adaptations that arose in response to difficult circumstances. When we examine mental health struggles from this trauma-informed lens, we can understand the "why" behind the behaviors. As a therapist, IFS allows me to trust that the folks I work with already have what they need within them to heal. As a client and someone who uses IFS for herself, it allows me to trust myself in my own healing.

♡ Reflection

What old messages do you carry that can be shifted to parts language? Think of a negative or painful message you hold about yourself. Notice how it feels when you state this message as if it is a fact, such as "I always make mistakes." Notice how it feels when you shift this to parts language: "A part of me makes mistakes" or "A part of me believes I always make mistakes."

EXERCISE

Parts Circular Timeline

In IFS, we acknowledge that we each inherently possess Self-energy, but in response to difficult events or interactions with others, parts form and begin to do certain jobs within the system. Parts form like shells around our Self-energy, blocking us from accessing it. In order to get to know some of your parts, I invite you to fill in these circles with pivotal events that have occurred in your life, including an approximate age at which the event transpired and a description of the parts that developed in response. For example, perhaps at age 5 your parents went through a separation that caused an anxiety part to develop. Or maybe at age 12 a people-pleasing part formed when you started at a new school. This exercise will allow you to get to know your system and develop more awareness around which parts protect it.

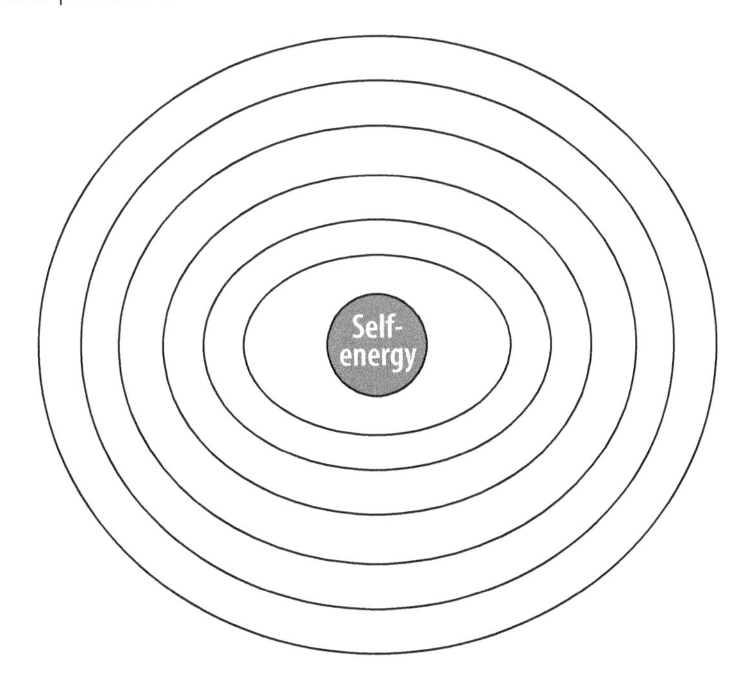

TRAUMA AND IFS

Though we are just beginning, we have already touched lightly on the concept of trauma. Before moving further, I want to share more about the definition of trauma and its relation to IFS. When people initially think about trauma, they often imagine a frightening or life-threatening event. Perhaps the word brings to mind a car accident, an assault, or a natural disaster. While these events can certainly lead to trauma, it is not the event itself that defines trauma. Rather, trauma is a physiological response to any threat or distress, whether perceived or real. When we perceive something in our environment as threatening, the amygdala—which we can think of as the brain's alarm bell—sends a signal for the nervous system to launch into a threat response. This threat response is intended to aid in our survival and can involve moving into one of four different reactionary modes: fight, flight, freeze, or fawn.

In *fight* mode, we attempt to ward off the threat by facing it head-on and fighting back. This reactionary mode represents a state of mobilization where we are energized to take action. However, if the threat seems too overwhelming, we can move into the *flight* response instead, in which we attempt to run away from or escape the perceived threat. Both fight and flight reflect a state of nervous system hyperarousal in which our bodies are filled with adrenaline and cortisol, propelling us toward action.

However, our threat response system can also move us into a state of hypoarousal, in which the nervous system slows us down rather than energizes us. Our bodily functions shut down as we move toward a state of immobilization, often with no access to speech or cognitive function. This is known as the *freeze* response. Sometimes this looks like dissociation or exhaustion, while other times it looks like stillness or the act of a deer in headlights. In this state, we may "play dead" against the perceived predator as a means of survival.

Finally, the fourth reactionary mode is the *fawn* response, in which we bend to the needs of others and sacrifice our own needs in order to stay safe (Walker, 2013). This response happens in a state of social engagement and often manifests as a form of people-pleasing behavior. In infancy, this can involve forgoing our own needs to engage with our caregivers. For example, if our hunger cues are ignored or met with annoyance, we might suppress them. In adult years, this can involve sacrificing our own needs in a relationship as a way to ensure that we maintain connection. It can also involve appeasing a perpetrator who is coercing us into unwanted sexual acts because pleasing them feels safer than saying no. Unlike fight, flight, and freeze, which have been with us since birth, the fawn response may develop relationally later in life.

These threat responses all occur subconsciously, before the conscious mind has time to register what is happening. As a result, we are often unable to make sense of the stimulus that caused the reaction. After the event is over, we may struggle to remember specific details of the trauma as well. That's because trauma does not simply live in the brain. It is also stored in our body in the form of somatic memories that can show up as unexplained pain, tension, fatigue, discomfort, or other physical symptoms. Traumatic events that occur in early childhood, before we develop the capacity for language, are often stored as somatic memories. For these reasons, traditional talk therapy taps into only a portion of the story and heals only pieces of the system.

Importantly, the nervous system treats *any* potential threat as a life-or-death situation. That means it will react the same way to your spouse raising their voice as it would if a bear were coming into your field of vision. However, as we know, trauma does not just occur as a result of distressing events; the nervous system can also register trauma from a lack of a healthy attachment with our earliest caregivers. As infants and young children, we require connection to let us know that the world is a safe place. When we don't receive this connection—perhaps our caregivers were abusive, neglectful, or walled-off emotionally—it leads us to perceive the world as unsafe. In turn, our threat response sends signs of distress in an attempt to get our core needs met.

Regardless of its origin, trauma causes disorganization to the system. Even after the trauma is long over, the nervous system remains hypersensitive to threat, leading it to react to any stimuli that even remotely remind us of the trauma. These are known as "trauma triggers," and they cause the nervous system to launch into a threat response, even if at a conscious level we know there is no real threat present. This is where parts can develop, as they reflect an attempt to reorganize the system following trauma. Some parts develop to help us respond to triggers, while others aid us in organizing the system or achieving coherence. Some parts may also act as protectors, always trying to remain one step ahead to ensure the trauma won't happen again.

Then there are parts that are most touched by trauma, who may feel as though they are stuck close to it, unable to orient back to safety. These parts carry the burdens our trauma leaves behind. Although we often turn away from these most burdened parts—believing that they are bad or wrong, or that they get in the way—

understanding these parts as adaptations to what we have endured can help in building compassion for them. Rather than turning away, we can create more space to get to know them. Often, they simply want to be heard, as many of these parts have been doing their job for a long time without any recognition for their hard work. As these parts feel heard and welcomed—rather than feared or shunned—they actually ease and soften, allowing more information about our inner world to unfold. When we turn toward them with acceptance and understanding, we can provide them with the loving compassion that *all* our parts (especially those closest to the trauma) so deserve.

As you continue this journey into a deeper understanding of yourself, you may meet parts that you didn't know were there. Some may feel difficult or scary to get to know. You may uncover new information those parts are holding. You may touch into places that feel especially raw or tender. To help you feel secure throughout this journey, I invite you to try the following exercise, which encourages you to build a safe container that can house your parts as you look within yourself. Whenever the content becomes too intense and awakens too much, know that you have built this safe container to return to when needed.

EXERCISE

Building a Home for Your Parts

I invite you to close your eyes, if that feels good to you, while you settle into a comfortable position. This is the beginning of our journey. At this time, you may not have any awareness of parts, or perhaps you've met some before. It's okay either way. As you journey through this book, you may become aware of your parts. Before you meet them, we are going to establish a container to keep them safe when needed. This is a container you can return to at any time.

Imagine a building or structure in which your parts can reside. Perhaps it is a house or apartment building. Perhaps it is a cabin or tent. Perhaps it is a nondescript location or perhaps someplace you know and feel comfortable. Imagine this place has a room for each of your parts and the ability to add new rooms when needed. You don't need to picture the rooms yet, but just know they will be available when needed. This is a structure for your parts only. You have full control over who comes in and out.

Imagine the environment that surrounds your structure. It can be real or imagined. Perhaps it is in a quiet forest or a loud city. Perhaps the structure is surrounded by a beach, or even by clouds. As you notice the environment of your structure, imagine details that ignite your senses. What do you see? Hear? Feel? Smell?

As you imagine the details of your structure—the home for your parts—notice any sensations that arise in your body. Do you feel a warmth in your chest? A settling in your shoulders? Bubbling in your stomach? Tingling in your hands? Focus in on the sensation, allowing a word to come to mind that could represent this home for your parts. With this word in mind, you can easily return to your home when needed. This home offers containment as you move through connection with your parts. This is a place to return to when parts arise throughout this book and through your process of connecting with them.

2

Parts of You

There is a part within me that helps me shut down. When the conversation becomes too much, when the overwhelm becomes too great, the shutdown part overtakes me. It seems to spread throughout my whole body, centering in my chest and making me feel frozen in my body. When I check in with this part, it prefers not to give me any information at all. I let it know that that's okay, that I'm not going to push it too far or ask it not to do its job. This allows it to relax a bit. I can feel my breath flowing more freely as it relaxes. It feels like an old part, one that's served me for a long time. I ask when it first showed up. It shows me images of getting in trouble as a child. I feel a sinking of shame. My head and neck begin to feel heavy. I ask how it would feel about not having to do its job anymore. The freezing sensation grows stronger once again, making my body feel heavy. It's not ready yet.

Perhaps this is your first introduction to parts. Some of us have always had awareness of our parts, and naming and recognizing this facet of multiplicity within us feels natural. For others, the concept of parts may feel confusing or strange. Wherever you land on this spectrum, this chapter will aid in defining and helping you to recognize your own parts.

Have you ever erupted with anger at someone and felt as though you were unable to stop it? Perhaps it sounded like the anger came from a disembodied voice that didn't feel like your own. You might have felt some guilt as you heard the words come out of your mouth, but you still felt unable to stop them. When the other person responded to your wrath, you struggled to pause and take in what they were saying; instead, the anger seemed to grow. It took over those feelings of guilt that were lingering in the background until the anger stood alone. When the angry spell finally diminished, you found yourself alone and settled. Maybe you noticed the guilt returning—fueling shame that stirred the anger once again. You might have then come down on yourself, the anger turning inward.

This description of anger may feel familiar. For many of us, this angry behavior results in feelings of shame, causing us to hold narratives such as "I'm a bad person." However, through the lens of parts work, we can look at the multiplicity present within the description and instead, form a different narrative when an event like this happens. From an IFS perspective, you merely became *blended* with the angry part, which is a word that describes what happens when a part takes over (Schwartz, 2021). A guilty part then came online in an attempt to calm the angry part. When the other person reacted to your response, the angry part grew, causing it to further blend with your system. Once the confrontation was over, the angry part began to *unblend*—a word we use in IFS to describe a part softening, stepping back, and allowing in Self-energy—and the shame part presented itself. This part attempted to turn the anger inward to diminish the outward behavior associated with anger.

After acknowledging the inner experience of anger through an IFS lens, how do you feel toward the angry part? Often, delving deeper into the role of a part allows us to offer some compassion or care toward it. This allows us more space to learn about the part. The experience of parts may feel different for each person, but they are all entities that exist within us, acting as pieces of our inner world. While they may represent emotions, memories, behaviors, body sensations, jobs, roles, and more, they also hold their *own* emotions, memories, behaviors, body sensations, jobs, and roles. These entities feel distinct once we turn our attention toward them, and when we focus on them, we can experience the messages and information they hold.

Tuning into parts is a way to listen more deeply to our internal world. If at first, we aren't aware of our parts, we can activate them by directing questions toward them and bringing them forward through meditation. We can welcome and communicate with these parts as the separate entities that they are—acknowledging them and showing appreciation and compassion for the jobs they do. The bridge of connection between us and our parts is not made in an attempt to eradicate the parts altogether, but as we start to get in touch with them, we learn to build greater Self-trust and acknowledge our innate capacity for healing. While it is often a therapist who initiates parts work, or the voice of the trusty narrator within this book (yours truly), the facilitator is simply the guide to the internal experience. The rest happens within you.

EXERCISE

Meeting Your Parts

I invite you to close your eyes if that feels okay. Allow your body to relax or be at rest, as much as feels pleasant, in whatever way "relax" lands for you. As you allow your body to do this, notice whether any body parts are holding tension, or whether any areas are holding pleasant sensations. If any areas are holding tension, check in to see what the tension might need from you in order to release or soften. Is there anything the tension wants you to know? What about those body parts that are holding pleasant sensations? Notice how the sensations show up for you—perhaps as a warmth or calmness. What do the pleasant sensations want you to know? Is there any information they are holding? Are they able to expand? Perhaps they can offer this pleasantness to the areas filled with tension.

As you continue allowing your body to relax, notice whether any emotions or thoughts arise. If so, see if it's okay to focus your attention there, just being with the emotion or thought without trying to move or change it. As you stay with it, notice if it moves or changes on its own. Just watch and notice. Does the emotion or thought show up in or around your body? If you can feel it, what's the sensation like? Does it have a temperature or texture? A consistency? Does it feel as though it overtakes you, or is it centered in one area? Does an image arise? Continue to stay with this part of you a few more moments, without judgment and without any intention to move or change it. Then thank this part for coming forward today.

If you notice that this exercise is difficult, perhaps another part of you is coming in. Thank that part for coming forward today. If you're able, send it some gratitude and compassion,

and notice how it takes that in. Allow this part to choose a room within your house of parts, staying there until you're able to connect with it next.

EXERCISE

Parts in the Body

To locate parts within your body, do a body scan, bringing your attention to the top of your head and gradually moving down your body. Work your way through your neck, shoulders, arms, chest, seat, thighs, and legs until you reach your feet. As you scan through, tune into any sensations and parts that arise in your body. Use the outline here, or create your own, to identify where these parts show up. Use a different color to represent each part, adding a word to represent the sensations associated with this part.

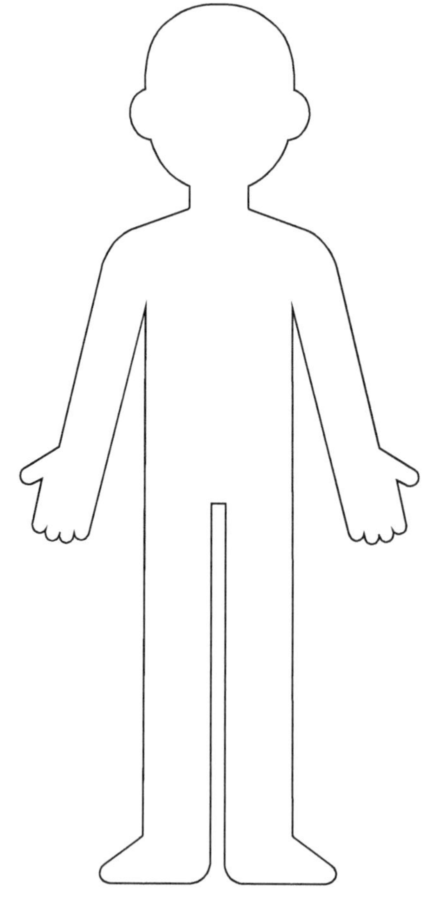

DISCOVERING MY OWN PARTS

In my graduate program at St. Edwards University, I was lucky to have select professors and mentors who were well versed in trauma. During my second semester, I met Dr. Sunny Lansdale, who was a wise and loving presence. She was a woman in her seventies with gray hair—and the quintessential therapist "look" I'd always pictured. She stayed up to date on the latest trauma research, and I wanted to soak in every word she said. I'd never heard anyone speak about trauma this way before. She introduced us to the work of Daniel Siegel, Peter Levine, Bonnie Badenoch, and Richard Schwartz. Their words sounded like poetry to me, and suddenly trauma (and my responses to my own trauma) made so much sense.

It was in Sunny's class that I first learned of the concept of parts. As she spoke, I could feel the young parts of myself stirring inside. They were inner children I'd pushed deep down to protect—parts who were 10, 15, 17, and even 22 years old. I was never one to volunteer for class exercises, but as I watched Sunny demonstrate parts work with a student who was meeting their own young parts, I felt settled knowing that I could feel my own parts stirring inside. I volunteered to participate in the next training session, and it was during this training that I truly met my own parts for the first time.

As I sat across from my partner that first day of doing experiential work, I didn't know what to expect. She was nervous and gripped her paper. As she began to prompt me, I felt a stirring inside. A sensation began to form in my chest and stomach. The sensation felt like a heavy bubbling energy, and my body felt as though it was swaying. I closed my eyes to stay with the sensation.

"What does that part want you to know?" my partner asked.

As I felt the sway, an image of the ocean came to me. I saw the sun glistening on the water and myself floating in the vastness. I reported this to my partner, continuing to stay with the image and sensation.

"I need a vacation," I said, with tears forming in my eyes.

She turned to the assistant who was supporting our group and asked, "Is this okay? Should I keep going?"

I sensed that my partner was scared by my tears. Whenever I felt like I was causing others to experience discomfort, I typically had parts come online, or blend with me, to let me know that I was "too much." However, in this moment, I felt another part step in instead—a protector. This part entered in to support me so my partner's part wouldn't interfere with my experience. I felt as though this protector was whispering to me, "It's okay." I didn't report this, though I felt it. I said out loud, "It's okay," and my partner's own parts stepped to the side, allowing her to come back to presence with mine.

In turn, I was able to move more deeply toward my own parts. With this new access and understanding of my internal experience, I was able to come to my own aid rather than dragging myself down with old messages. I held compassion for my partner, who was experiencing this therapy modality for the first time *and* could offer compassion to my own parts. I was beginning to understand the magic of IFS and the beauty of it being facilitated by a therapist, while it deepened my connection with myself.

As therapists, we learn modalities by practicing with each other. We know that going into a training session, we will be doing our own inner work. I have parts that adore this facet of being a therapist and parts that dread it. My therapist part knows that with any work

I'm doing with clients, I must fully believe in myself. I cannot take clients to depths within their own systems that I have not been to within *my* own.

TOUCHING INTO PARTS

As you have learned, our parts are pieces of consciousness within us, some more potent than others. The experience of touching into these parts may feel different for different people. Some people may experience parts as sensations, images, messages, or all of these together. Other people might experience parts as entities existing inside of them.

My own experience of feeling my parts typically begins with noticing a body sensation. As I focus on the sensation, I allow my rational, analytical brain to take a backseat. I listen only to the messages coming through my body. Whenever my rational, analytical brain tries to step in, I consider this to be another part coming through and ask it to step to the side. This is a unique facet of IFS—whereas traditional talk therapy emphasizes being able to access our rational brain, IFS allows us to let go of the analytical parts and receive messages from within. As I tune into these messages, I typically feel a shift in my body sensations first and then become aware of images and messages coming through. Your own experience may differ as you learn your own internal makeup. Perhaps you'll notice messages or images first. Perhaps you'll notice something entirely different. Perhaps it will feel difficult to access parts at all.

As you become more aware of what it feels like to tune into your parts, you will become increasingly aware of what it feels like when a part takes over—not in the sense that it takes over your consciousness but in the sense that it feels as though you're being led by a part. You'll recall from earlier in this chapter that this is known as *blending* (Schwartz, 2021), and it occurs when a part becomes so enmeshed in the system that it becomes indistinguishable from the Self. In this state, we lose access to Self-energy, and our rational thinking goes offline. In my own life, a prime example of blending occurs when I am reactive toward my husband. When I am in Self-energy, I am able to take in what my husband is saying and respond with compassion. However, when I am blended with a part, I perceive my husband through the lens of that part. For example, I may take in a past version of him, perceive him as a parent figure instead of a husband, or assume that his message is about me rather than him. Because the part is online and I am perceiving my spouse through this part, I might respond with anger or frustration, words that harm, or body language that shows disrespect.

> *There is a part of me that holds shame around money. It gets stirred in response to my spouse. My husband questions me about bills and the part becomes frantic. I feel my heart rate pick up, and my head rushes with thoughts. My legs feel the urge to run but are frozen at the same time. My eyes look straight ahead, unable to meet his. My face becomes flushed. I feel a sense of panic within. As I check in with the part, I feel its terror. I have an image of it shrinking as the terror takes over. I let it know that I'm not trying to hurt it, that I am here, and that I am safe. I am going to stay with it before we decide to respond.*
>
> *As I stay with it, I feel the wave of shame. This part is worried that it may be in trouble. I let it know that we're not in trouble and ask it how old it thinks I am. Its response comes through: 16 years old. I give it a small update—that I'm 34 and*

that my impulsiveness around money has subsided a great deal. I let it know that my husband just wants to check in on bills so we're staying ahead of things. That he's not mad at us, that we're just having a serious conversation. I feel some relief coming from the part, which shows up as a softening in my chest and a slowing down of my heart rate. It's willing to ease to allow me to converse with my husband. I feel my jaw loosen, and I have access to my voice once again. The shutdown has subsided. The part is willing to step back to allow me to engage once again.

As you become more aware of your parts, you'll be able to notice and check in prior to becoming blended with a part (and assist parts in the process of unblending when you do). Often, when you are reacting to a situation from the point of view of a part, there is a greater need that lays beneath the surface. Perhaps a harsh response with a partner is a part who wants to be heard. When you can tend to those needs prior to responding, you can aid the part in unblending and offer it Self-energy.

EXERCISE

Freewriting with a Part

Think of a part who has been making itself known to you lately, whether it's been arising in your interactions with others or showing up internally. As you bring this part to mind, allow yourself to write from the perspective of this part for 10 minutes without your pen leaving the paper. You can use the space below to begin with and then continue writing in a journal. When you're finished freewriting, read over what has come forward, allowing yourself to reflect on the point of view of this part.

TYPES OF PARTS

According to IFS, there are three different types of parts that can make up our internal system: managers, firefighters, and exiles. Managers and firefighters are both types of protective parts in that their main job is to keep our more vulnerable parts, known as exiles, from experiencing any pain or suffering. Our exiles are the parts of us that are burdened from the traumatic experiences of our past, usually in childhood, and they can overwhelm the system when they become activated. Therefore, protective parts work overtime to keep these exiles under the surface and out of consciousness, even if their methods for doing so can sometimes be extreme.

Manager Parts

Managers are protective parts that attempt to defend us against any potential harm that could conceivably arise in the future. They do so by trying to control everything in our everyday lives so we can avoid experiencing trauma, pain, humiliation, or rejection ever again. Although these parts have the best of intentions and believe they're doing an important job to keep us safe, they are also the parts that may frustrate us the most. Managers may show up as perfectionistic parts, critical parts, or people-pleasing parts—to name a few.

Managers often develop from a young age, which correlates with their role in protecting the young, exiled parts within us. In getting to know our managers and releasing them from the difficult job they have been doing, we can get to know the exiled parts they've been protecting. However, we should not push past protective parts to get deeper within the system, even if we are eager to meet exiles. When we try to move forward in healing without checking in with our managers, this can cause pushback, where they come on stronger and *more* protective of the young ones, like parents protecting their children from a stranger.

Firefighter Parts

Firefighters are also protective parts, but unlike managers, they are reactive in that they only emerge once some pain or trauma has broken through the surface. It is the goal of firefighters to get rid of that pain as quickly as possible—to put out the fire. Firefighters are more likely to show up as extreme behaviors that can manifest as substance use, disordered eating, self-harm, and impulsivity. Dissociative parts can also manifest as firefighters. We often feel shame around these parts because it can feel as though we have no control over them. But just like managers, when we get to know them, they too can ease up—allowing us to get to the root of the pain and heal from a deeper place—so they no longer have to do their job as intensely.

Exiled Parts

Finally, exiles are the parts that live deepest within us. They lie beneath the many layers of protectors and hold our deepest wounds. Exiles are the parts that were closest to the trauma and that still carry the associated burdens of shame, rejection, fear, and pain. Exiles have been pushed deep down for protection because they hold information that we are not yet ready to endure or face. These exiled parts often represent different versions of ourselves, including different ages or stages of our lives. Eventually, the goal of IFS is to unburden the exiles and release them from the pain they have been carrying. When we are in a state of Self-energy, we can aid the exiles in finding safety and let them know the trauma of the past has subsided (Schwartz, 2021).

SELF-ENERGY

Along with parts, we all possess Self-energy, which you'll recall is a feeling of centeredness. From a neurobiological perspective, we are in Self-energy when our nervous system is at rest and we have access to safety and security within us. We know we're in Self-energy when we can embody the following qualities, which Schwartz (2021) describes as the 8 C's:

1. Curiosity
2. Calm
3. Connectedness
4. Confidence
5. Clarity
6. Compassion
7. Courage
8. Creativity

These eight qualities represent what we strive for to become more Self-led—one of the goals of IFS—which means that we are building a greater capacity for Self-energy. When we feel these qualities, we fill the well of Self-energy, allowing us to offer it to our parts to pull from when we have access to it. In this state, we can offer them a sense of safety and security and can better attune to what is happening within us and outside of us.

♡ *Reflection*

As we begin to name the types of parts, do you notice anything arise within you? Do your own parts begin to unfold, feeling ignited by these categories? Do you notice parts that show up more or less often? What happened for you with the mention of the "Self"? Are you able to connect with the Self inside of you? If not, what feels like it may be blocking this connection?

THE 6 F'S

In getting to know our protective parts and becoming more Self-led, we turn toward the 6 F's to help us better understand our parts' goals and motives. It is important to remember that, at their core, protective parts are simply trying to guard against the pain and suffering that the exiles carry. By using the 6 F's as a guide, we can get to know these parts and help them unblend from the Self, which allows us to gain better access to the underlying exiles they are protecting. The basic steps involved in the 6 F's are as follows:

1. **Find**: Direct your attention inward to determine where the part shows up in or around the body. Recall that parts often show up as physical sensations, images, messages, or all of these together.
2. **Focus**: Offer curiosity toward the part. What do you notice as you turn your attention toward the part? Does anything shift or change about the part?

3. **Flesh it out**: See what else you notice about the part or what information it offers you. For example, you might be able to see an image of what the part looks like. Or you might receive information about what the part is holding about itself and your connection to it.
4. **Feel**: Notice how you feel about this part with the information you have. This lets you know the extent to which you are in Self-energy with this part. If you feel anything other than the 8 C's toward this part, then this is an indication that you are blended with another protective part. In this case, it is important to see if this second protective part is willing to step back so you can have enough Self-energy to continue exploring the first protective part.
5. **BeFriend**: Just as you would a friend, allow yourself to get to know this part and for this part to get to know you. Further delve into the story of the part: When did it first show up? What does it believe its job is? This allows you to build appreciation and learn more about its history.
6. **Fear**: Find out what the part fears would happen if it were to stop doing its job. When you understand what the part is afraid of, you can better appreciate why it likely doesn't want to give up its job. Most parts formed to combat fear of some kind, and this helps you better understand why they formed within your system.

Throughout this book, many of the exercises utilize the 6 F's to aid us in getting to know our parts. It may feel strange or frightening at first, as we begin to communicate with ourselves—or past versions of ourselves—but becoming aware of our parts is a beautiful and powerful experience. It can shift how we interact with others and ourselves. When we do get to a point where our parts become unburdened and unblended, the entire system will feel more coordinated. And though the parts may become unblended, they will always be inside of us. I find comfort in knowing that when I feel nostalgic for a past version of myself, she is not gone or forgotten. I can still access her and be with her by tending to that part of me. When I yearn to experience a time in my life with the knowledge I have now, I can access that part of me, updating her on the knowledge I hold now, celebrating the strides I've made, and tending to her in the ways she needed at the time.

EXERCISE

Non-Dominant Hand Drawing

Drawing with your non-dominant hand (the hand you don't usually write with) allows you to access the right brain, which is where your emotions and subconscious are held. To begin, bring up a part you'd like to get to know better. Imagine a time this part showed up for you. Notice where it's located in your body and if any image arises with the sensation. Once you locate the part in your body, allow your hands to let that part appear on paper. Draw whatever arises in the space below or on a separate sheet of paper. What do you notice about how the part appeared? Should any judgmental or critical parts arise, ask them to step to the side so you're able to be only with the part you're drawing on the paper.

3

Manager Parts

There is a part of me that believes I'm going to die. It constricts my throat, making it difficult to breathe. In that constriction, I hear it say, "We're going to die." I feel worry toward this part—worry that if I don't listen, my fate will be sealed. I focus in on the constriction and notice my heart rate rising. I let the part know that I can feel my pulse coming in strong, so I don't think we're dying. It doesn't believe me. It doesn't ease up. I begin to feel fear toward this part. It feels difficult to be with. I let the part know this, and I feel it ease just a bit.

I check in to ask this part how long it's been around. It shows me a 14-year-old me. It shows me an image of that younger me watching the Twin Towers fall on TV at school. She looks confused. I have an impulse to move toward the young me, and as I do, my heart rate intensifies again and my throat constricts further. It makes sense to me that this part first showed up at that time, and I let it know that. I feel a shiver, acknowledging the difficulty of that year.

I ask the part what it's afraid might happen if it wasn't there to do its job. It is afraid I'll die. I acknowledge this and ask the

> *part if it knows that it makes me feel as though I'm going to die. It was not aware. I ask the part what it might need to not come on so strong. "For you to hear me," it says. I let it know that I can hear it and that I will hear it. I ask the part if, next time it comes on so strong, I can ask it to turn down the volume so I can listen more intently, rather than being in a panic. It agrees. I thank it and place my hands on my heart, sending compassion toward this one.*

I have a lot of managers within my system. It feels as though each time I make strides with one, another shows up. They beg for my attention, though they feel difficult to get to know. When I think of the managers within my system, I think about Dwight Schrute from the television show *The Office*, played by actor Rainn Wilson. He calls himself Assistant Regional Manager, though his boss, Michael Scott, is quick to correct him: "Assistant *to* the Regional Manager" (Daniels et al., 2005–2013). I view my managers as mini Dwight Schrutes in that they each take their jobs very seriously, relish being in control, and spring into action during times of crisis—but as I get to know and understand them better, and they feel heard, they are more able to ease.

HOW MANAGERS SHOW UP

Managers may feel difficult to get to know because they can come on strong and show up as parts that bring discomfort. They can also cause me to display behaviors I'm not proud of, especially in relational dynamics. In my own work with managers, I have found it helpful to shift my language to identify them as protectors. When I can acknowledge these parts as protectors, I make more room to understand why the behaviors have shown up alongside these parts. This allows me to offer more softness and compassion toward them.

As you learned in the last chapter, parts develop in response to difficult situations or trauma we have endured. Managers, in particular, show up not only to ensure that the trauma doesn't happen again, but to protect exiled parts from enduring further trauma. Toward this end, the goal of managers is to keep our exiles from being awakened or activated because if they do come to the surface, they may believe the trauma is happening again (Schwartz, 2021). Managers will come on strong to ensure that doesn't happen.

As part of doing this job, managers engage in a variety of behaviors they believe to be protective. Sometimes these behaviors appear good and helpful on the surface even though they hinder us in other ways. For example, managers can show up as perfectionistic, controlling, or workaholic parts that help us excel at our jobs, but this can also lead to burnout and imbalance. Sometimes managers show up in a way that doesn't seem to aid our functioning, but there is usually a protective role when we look deeper. For example, depressed parts may appear to keep us stuck and interfere with productivity, but when we get to know these parts, we might find their job is to protect us from the intensity of difficult emotions. Anxious parts also show up often as managers. While they too feel inconvenient and inhibitive in the moment, when we get to know them, we often find that they are attempting to manage future dangers by presenting them as worries. In fact, most of our managers are future-focused since they take a proactive approach in keeping exiles at bay.

Manager Behaviors

- Depression
- Tuning out
- Toxic positivity
- Self-criticism
- Controlling
- Overachieving
- Mothering
- Overworking
- Being a good child
- Turning inward
- Technology dependence
- Perfectionism
- Overcompensating
- Underfunctioning
- Advice giving
- Anxiety
- People pleasing
- Helping
- Overfunctioning
- Approval seeking
- Emotional wall
- Self-doubt
- Intellectualizing
- Judging
- Invalidating
- Self-sacrificing
- Masking
- Pessimism
- Self-blaming
- Focusing on others

Managers hinder us because in their attempt to protect us from one aspect of the present moment, they often block us from being present at all. When we recognize these hinderances, we often experience frustration. *Why can't this manager just step to the side or stop doing its job so I can better function?* This frustration often causes managers to come on more strongly. They feel their job is at risk and must work harder to keep the system functioning. My people-pleasing part is a difficult one to contend with. Though I can understand the reasons she shows up and why she stands so firm, she is a part I struggle to feel compassion for. But she is also a part who needs compassion the most. She believes she helps me keep friendships, makes me a good mother and partner, and most importantly, keeps me safe. She is deeply tied to my identity and trauma as a female. I know that if I show this part more ease, she will feel it and allow ease in return. But I also know I can't force this ease; she must accept it on her own.

There is a people-pleasing part of me who fears standing up for herself, so she gives in to the needs of others. She makes sure everyone is comfortable and happy but often forgets to ensure this for herself. Her needs fade into the background and often are forgotten. She abandons them so often that other people often forget she has any. I feel sadness toward this part. Along with the sadness comes frustration. This part exhausts me. She is quick to overtake me, leaving me with hunger, exhaustion, and the ability to do little more than lay in bed. She's afraid that if she stopped doing her job, I would no longer be a good mother, partner, or friend. If she were to let me admit that I'm tired or lonely, it would be too much for others to handle.

Though this part comes on strong in motherhood and with my current relationships, I ask when she first showed up. She shows me an image of a scared 17-year-old, laying frozen beneath a Mickey Mouse blanket in the basement of her home. She shows me images of the morning after, when the 17-year-old kissed her assaulter blankly, hoping he would just leave. As the people-pleasing part shows me these images, I feel angry toward her. I let her know this, and my chest grows hot. She cowers but doesn't leave. The warmth grows more intense and unpleasant. The part feels fearful of my anger. She lets me know, and I breathe deeply and move through it. It is not her I'm angry at.

I can understand her. That she tried to protect me by shrinking and silencing me, that it was the best she could do at the time. I let her know. Another part comes in and says, "She's the reason we were assaulted in the first place." My eyes fill with tears.

Our managers often have very noble causes. The way they show up may feel productive or even essential to our functioning. They can slip under the radar because they show up to keep us working, to keep us showing up in relationships, to keep us driven. It can be hard to tell that we are functioning from a manager part, or difficult to think about relieving a manager part of its job, because we have learned to fiercely depend on it. I think of my own people pleaser—she showed up intensely at a time when my body and well-being were in danger. She believed that if I didn't bend to my assaulter, I would be in further danger. She also believes that she keeps me likeable and protects me from the shame I may endure should I make the wrong move. She believes she keeps me from hurting others.

However, I know this is a part that I function from, rather than a quality I have, because it also exhausts me. My people pleaser suppresses my own needs in favor of others. She keeps my boundaries wavering and loose. She favors my protection over my comfort. She fears being wrong. She struggles to say no and often gives beyond her needs (physically, emotionally, and monetarily).

♡ Reflection

As we begin to acknowledge the role of managers, can you feel any of your own managers coming forward? Can you recognize the ways they have shown up to protect you? How have these attempts to help become a hindrance? As you acknowledge the ways your managers seek to help, are you able to offer some gratitude toward these parts?

GETTING TO KNOW YOUR MANAGERS

It is common to experience resistance at the idea of getting to know our managers. There are many reasons for this. First, our managers have served us for a long time and have helped us in many ways. Getting to know them may feel like we're letting them go, and it can be hard to let go of something that feels so familiar. In addition, we may worry that if a manager shifts or changes the way it works, it means we too will change. There can be fear in this. For example, in working with a manager such as a perfectionist part, we may fear that if we unburden that part, we will begin to make many mistakes.

Resistance can also *be* a manager. If resistance is a part who shows up and struggles to step to the side, we must get to know that part first. We must let it know that by encouraging it to ease its job, we are not asking it to go away or even diminish its role. We are simply getting to know it better. We are building trust with this part so we can better understand its role within the system. With this understanding, we can offer compassion to this part, which naturally allows more ease to come through. Remember that when our parts feel like they are being heard, we build trust that lets them know we can tend to the exiles and keep them out of harm's way.

EXERCISE

Getting to Know a Manager

Go inside yourself for a moment, noticing what this chapter might have brought up within you so far. Perhaps there is a manager you'd like to get to know better. Or maybe a manager has been awakened for you as you resonated with this chapter.

You can also think of a recent situation when a manager was online. Notice how you functioned from this part in the moment. What did it look like to be blended with this part? What behaviors did you exhibit? How did it hinder you in the moment? How did it help you? If you cannot think of anything recent, consider what parts might show up often to help you in your day-to-day life. What roles do you hold that require the help of a manager? What behaviors do you exhibit that reflect manager behaviors?

Once you've identified a manager, notice what it feels to acknowledge that part. Where does it arise in or around your body? How do you feel toward this part? As you notice how you feel, what shows up in your body? Do you feel a resistance or ease? Do you feel a curiosity? How do you feel about getting to know it better?

Now consider how this part functions for you. What does this part believe its job to be? What are the ways it believes it is helpful? What hopes and fears does this part hold? How does it protect you from those fears?

As you notice the ways this part believes it is helpful, are you able to send it compassion? If not, what is blocking the compassion from coming through? Perhaps this is another manager showing up. Check in and see if this new manager is able to step to the side in order to get to know the initial manager you're working with. Once the new manager steps to the side, ask what the initial manager needs from you in order to take in the compassion. Is this something you're able to offer? If not, imagine that you are able to simply send gratitude toward this part. Thank it for coming forward and allowing you to deepen your relationship with it. If you're able, make a plan to check in with this one again to deepen your connection with it and get to know it better.

EXERCISE

Journal Prompt for a Resistant Part

Grab a writing utensil if you are able, and settle into a comfortable position. As you've touched into your parts so far, have you noticed any parts arise in opposition or resistance to your exploration? If so, see if you can access them now. Notice where they're showing up in or around your body. Sometimes they can feel like a wall within the chest or a shortness of breath. Notice what happens for you.

When did this part first arise for you? If it was in response to getting to know another part, what fears does this one hold around you getting to know the other? Has this part shown up before in relation to other parts? As you tune in with these questions, allow yourself to write for three to five minutes from the perspective of this part. Write in the space below or on a separate sheet of paper. When your writing is complete, reflect on what you have written. What does it bring up in you? How is the part showing up in your body now?

MANAGER FEARS

In IFS, fear is considered the driving motivation behind each part. There are layers to this fear. In thinking about my own people pleaser, the outside layer of fear involves upsetting someone. When I move deeper with this part, I get to the ultimate fear: being alone. This part bends to others because she fears being alone. When I move even deeper, I can see that she is protecting an exile within me who holds this fear and who struggles with being alone.

Trauma survivors like myself have been touched by fear in a way that causes us to adapt to the world by either living in a constant state of fear or by becoming fearless. Each of these adaptations make sense. Constant fear means we think we are prepared for anything that comes our way. No fear means we are left unprepared when threat inevitably strikes. When we acknowledge managers as our first defense—as parts that assist us in functioning in response to the trauma we have endured—we can acknowledge the ways they prevent our fears from being realized. We can also acknowledge and explore the fears our managers have, which propel them to keep them doing their job so the fears don't come true.

Ultimately, our managers want to be recognized. They want to be acknowledged and heard. Even with those parts that feel the most detrimental, if we can get to know them and their purpose within the system, we can give them the support they need to soften. The hardest workers want the recognition they often don't receive. The ones that look like they're "fine" are the ones who are often left without recognition. If we can offer our managers the care they so desperately believe they're giving to us, we can hold the understanding and compassion these parts lack.

♡ Reflection

What came up for you as we referenced manager fears? Did you notice a part arise? If so, what fears or concerns does this part hold? When you touch into the fears, what do you notice in your body? What might this part need in order to move through the fear?

EXERCISE

Love Letter to a Manager

As we have established, our managers want to be heard and seen. As you conclude this chapter, I invite you to check in with a manager that comes online often for you. Can you feel it with you now? Notice where it is showing up in or around your body. As you locate this part, try offering compassion to it.

If there is anything that gets in the way of you offering compassion to this manager, there may be another part showing up. Check in with this new part and ask if there is anything it's needing from you. If it is willing, see if this part is able to gently step to the side so you can tend to the initial manager.

Returning to the chosen manager, see if you are able to now offer it compassion. For example, picture a circle of warmth around your heart and extend it out to this one. As you offer it compassion, allow your hands to choose a nearby writing utensil and piece of paper. Continuing to notice how this part is showing up in your body, write a love letter to your manager, acknowledging all the ways it shows up for you. Acknowledge the ways it has helped you function, kept you safe, and protected you.

When you're finished writing this letter, locate where the manager is showing up in or around your body now. As you experience the part within your body, read the letter back to the part, checking in with how it's received. Notice if any other parts show up in response and if they're able to gently step to the side so this manager can take in your love letter.

4

Firefighter Parts

There is a part of me that wants to die. It shows up in the depths of overwhelm—when I experience wounding from someone I love. The image is of a dark circle near my right shoulder. It is crouched alone in a dark corner. It is met with a sensation of stinging emptiness and the warmth of tears welling in my eyes. As I focus in on the sensation and image, I am fearful toward this part. I let it know, and the part strengthens, the dark circle growing bigger. I ask it if there is anything it wants me to know. "This is too much," it responds. I agree with it and feel the part taper off a tiny bit. It can feel me with it now. It allows me to stand with it but keeps me arm's length apart.

Next, I ask this part if it knows that if it dies, I will die with it. It was not aware, and I feel sadness coming from it now. "I don't want you to die," it says. I move closer toward it. I check in to see if it would be willing to ease so I can learn more about it. It would. It tells me it has been around since age 11 and shows me an image of my younger self from that time. For a moment, I feel that young one with me, and I try sending some tenderness toward her. The part who wants to die steps in,

> *blocking me from her. It believes it is protecting her. I let the part know that, should we die, this younger girl would die too. It softens further. I send some compassion toward it and witness it shifting from darkness to a glowing orb. My fear toward the part dissipates. It allows me to move closer, cradling it in my arms. "You are not alone," I let it know. "We are not alone."*

Our firefighters show up as a second line of defense, working to protect us from pain that has broken through the managers' defenses. Therefore, unlike managers, firefighters take a reactionary approach in that they attempt to put out flames caused by feelings of fear, loneliness, worthlessness, or shame. The goal of these parts is to put out the emotional fire as quickly as possible by providing some relief or comfort in the moment. When the brain is overwhelmed, it seeks a solution to the overwhelm. Firefighters hold easily accessible solutions.

HOW FIREFIGHTERS SHOW UP

In order to help us numb or kill the pain quickly, firefighters encourage us to engage in a variety of self-soothing behaviors, which can range from those that are socially acceptable in nature (such as exercising or numbing out in front of the television) to those that seem more extreme and drastic (like suicidality or substance use). Because we have been told some of these more extreme behaviors are bad or wrong, we can hold shame toward these parts, making it feel difficult or scary to get to know them.

Firefighter Behaviors

- Binge eating
- Drug use
- Suicidality
- Shoplifting
- Rage
- Self-harm
- Mindless scrolling
- Drinking
- Gambling
- Manipulation
- Dissociation
- Technology dependence
- Codependency
- Disordered eating
- Exercise
- Sleeping
- Compulsive sex
- Lying
- Running away
- Addiction
- Numbing out
- Abuse
- Hyper-independence
- Emotional cutoff
- Constant movement

Because some firefighters are not only detrimental, but deadly, we may feel a sense of urgency in unburdening these parts. In fact, as a therapist, I think about the fear I used to hold in working with the suicidal parts of clients. In graduate school, we are taught to come up with a crisis or safety plan when a client shares that they are suicidal. We are taught to ask them right away, "Do you have a plan?" to determine their risk. While it is important to take suicidal ideation and other life-threatening firefighters seriously, when you respond to a client as if their whole being is a firefighter (as opposed to just a part of them), it can cause the crisis to implode.

I know I have let down previous clients by presenting them with "crisis management" rather than humanity. My own managers arose in an attempt to protect the client's life that I feared was at risk. What our clients need in the midst of these tender and frantic parts being awakened is Self-energy—a calm anchor in the chaos. They need to feel our presence to know they are not alone. When instead, we meet them with crisis management, we move out of connection, which can in turn deepen the pain.

As I got to know my own parts through IFS, including a suicidal one, I recognized how my own urgency had fanned the flames of this firefighter part. As I got to know this part better, and was able to face it without fear, it was able to put down the firehose. This part was protecting a deep pain it didn't want me to get too close to. In reacting with fear or crisis, the firefighter worked harder, and the suicidal thoughts increased. When it was met with compassion and understanding, the overwhelm subsided.

♡ Reflection

As we touch into firefighters, do you notice any arising in your own system? Are you aware of the firefighters that show up most often for you? How have others responded to your firefighters in the past? How have you responded to your own firefighters in the past? After learning more about firefighters, how might you respond to them differently in the future?

GETTING TO KNOW YOUR FIREFIGHTERS

Just as managers require us to hear and turn toward them, so do firefighters. However, because firefighters come on intensely and are more likely to blend with the Self, it can feel difficult to get to know them. I have found it that the most effective way to become acquainted with firefighters is to do so when the part is offline or inactive. This is especially true for addictive parts. In the therapy room, we cannot conduct a session with a client who is actively under the influence. Similarly, we do not want to conduct our own self-work while under the influence of a firefighter who is active.

It is important to connect with firefighters because, even more so than managers, these parts get little recognition within the system. Most firefighter behaviors are frowned on from the outside world, so we learn to do the same. While we can acknowledge the harm they may cause, we can also give recognition to the ways they try to protect us. Often, firefighter parts don't even recognize the harm they cause within the system. It can be powerful to check in with a suicidal part only to find that it was not truly wanting to end or kill the system; rather, it was reacting against a certain part, trying to protect the system from feeling overwhelmed by offering an exit.

My own suicidal part showed up at 11 years old, a companion to the depressed parts that came on strong. As a preteen, I was so flooded with emotion that I didn't know what to do with it. It felt like I was always experiencing too much. Looking back, I can see that when I began to feel too much, the suicidal part showed up to let me know there was a way out of the intensity. I didn't share this with my therapist at the time (who would often treat my self-harm parts with shock and a call to my mom, who answered with, "I don't know what to do with this"), but I did tell other friends who had experienced similar feelings. My friends were able to meet my suicidal parts with understanding, and my suicidal part felt resonance in knowing that those friends had similar parts. We could meet one another in a place of compassion rather than crisis. In turn, the suicidal part felt seen and understood, as if it was allowed to be here.

This suicidal part has continued to show up at various points throughout my life, but much less so now. Still, when my brain gets overwhelmed, it makes itself known. As I've gotten to know this part better—acknowledging the ways it stepped in to protect that 11-year-old, 17-year-old, and 22-year-old—it has become less scary. I can respond as my friends did at the time, welcoming this part of me, no matter how darks it seems. It's funny, how when we welcome the parts of us who want to die, we suddenly see the light we couldn't before. A spark that shows us reason to live.

However, because firefighter parts are associated with so much shame, other protective parts commonly show up and block us from getting to know our firefighters. These protectors can show up as shame parts, fearful parts, anxious parts, or angry parts. These parts often hold judgments about firefighters and show up to prevent firefighters from acting on impulse. Unfortunately, these other protectors often exacerbate our firefighters, making them come on more strongly rather than cooling them down. Though firefighters can be detrimental, they ultimately believe they are protecting us—and when we make space to understand them, we can see the protection they offer. They simply act more urgently and potentially destructively than our manager parts.

EXERCISE

Getting to Know Protectors That Interfere with Firefighters

Think about a firefighter you'd like to get to know better—a part who tries to numb your pain. Think about the ways this part shows up for you. Imagine an instance or several instances that have awakened this part, perhaps uncomfortable emotions that show up before this part comes online or instances that cause this part to launch into action. Think about the last time this firefighter showed up for you. What did it look like? How did it affect you?

As you imagine this, notice what arises within you. There may be one or several parts that come forward. Notice each sensation that arises in your body as you begin to flesh out each part. For each part that comes forward, go through the following series of questions:

- What does this part want you to know about your firefighter?
- How does this part feel toward your firefighter?
- What fears does this part hold about this firefighter part becoming active?
- What fears does this part hold about you getting to know this firefighter?
- What does this part need to make space for you to get to know your firefighter?
- Is this part willing to hear what the firefighter has to say?
- Can you feel the firefighter responding to this part?
- If this part was able to listen to the firefighter, how does it feel toward it now?

- Invite this part to step to the side, while staying someplace nearby so it can step in if anything is needed.
- Thank this part for coming forward as it allows you to move closer to the firefighter.

EXERCISE

Getting to Know a Firefighter

Direct your awareness inside, and consider a firefighter part of you that comes online in an attempt to end your pain. As you think about this part, notice your capacity to be with it. If it feels difficult, perhaps allow yourself to feel into this part at whatever capacity feels okay to you, even if that is only .1% of yourself. Know that if it becomes too intense to be with this part, you can always thank it for coming forward and let it know that you'll return to it when you're able.

If you feel comfortable continuing, notice the sensations in your body as you create space to get to know this firefighter. Allow this part to feel you touching into that sensation. As you connect with this sensation and focus on it, how do you feel toward this part? Let the part know what you are feeling and notice what happens as a result.

Continue building a relationship with this part by asking when it first showed up for you. Can it offer an image or memory of that time? Be with this image or memory for as long or short as you need. As you're with this image or memory, what do you notice inside? Do you notice any shifts in how you're feeling toward this part? If your feelings have become less intense, let the firefighter know.

Next, ask the firefighter what it might need to let go of its job. What fears does it hold around letting this job come to an end? What does it need from you? Are you able to offer this to the part?

As you've learned about this part and its function, notice if anything has shifted in you. Then thank the part for coming forward and offer it a comfortable place to rest—perhaps a room within the house for your parts—until you can check in once again.

DISSOCIATIVE PARTS

For people who have endured immense trauma, typically from a young age, parts may show up with dissociative qualities that take over the driver's seat of consciousness. While dissociative parts can fit as managers and exiles, I am speaking about them here as firefighters because they fit the mold of stepping in to immediately put out the fire—to take the pain away—in favor of protecting exiles.

Dissociation is typically not a conscious behavior, and it can show up differently in different people. It reflects a type of trauma response—namely, the freeze response—that allows the brain to disconnect from a physically or emotionally overwhelming experience. For some, it feels like an out-of-body experience, and there may be the sensation of floating above their body. For others, it can feel like disconnection, as though things are happening around them but they are not present in the experience. Some describe the feeling of watching themselves, as though they are standing beside themselves or looking in on their own life. Still, for others, dissociation can show up as a sense of the world around them not being real. For many, dissociation is uncomfortable, even scary. While more awareness has been brought to dissociation in recent years, with greater access and awareness around trauma education, it can still be confusing to the person experiencing it and to those on the outside.

Because dissociative parts show up to help us diminish overwhelming feelings—or to calm the "too much" of trauma—we may have parts that try to tamper our dissociative parts, or that try to shame them in response; because of this, the mechanism may come on stronger. When we can instead acknowledge the ways that dissociative parts show up to "put out the fire" or diminish pain quickly and efficiently, we allow more space to get to know those parts and even welcome them. While we may not have much awareness while dissociative parts are online, we can still get to know them in the same way we can acquaint ourselves with other parts we have more conscious awareness of.

Although dissociation is another behavior that is frequently handled with a crisis response in the therapy room—especially if it shows up during the therapy session—we can't put out fire with fire. In these times, clinicians often speak about the importance of trying to aid clients in staying grounded. While grounding skills can be an effective antidote to dissociation, we need to be present with the dissociative parts and offer curiosity around why we're drifting into a dissociative state. With curiosity, we can begin to identify what awakens our dissociative parts and understand the ways they step in for us. With this understanding, we can gently begin to add in grounding and curiosity to relieve them of their jobs.

By getting to know our dissociative parts, we can get to a place where we no longer view them as extremes. This can also ease how we view our other firefighters, as well as the firefighters of those around us. When we can soften toward the parts that we once viewed as our darkest (and perhaps even our most dangerous), those parts gain the capacity to soften in return. It is beautiful to witness the unfolding of firefighters. Often, when we gently address the parts we fear the most—the parts that feel like they hold the greatest power—they actually loosen their grasp rather than tightening it. They slowly unburden from the system, knowing we will be okay without them. We will look at dissociative parts in more detail in chapter 9.

5

Exiled Parts

There is a part of me who is 10 years old. She feels confused and broken. Her feelings come on strong, with nowhere to go, so they explode out of her. The grown-ups don't understand it. They don't know what to do with her or what exactly is wrong. She still awakens sometimes in the face of her mom or others who don't seem to understand. Who face her as though she is broken. Who look her in the eyes and ask, "What's wrong with you?" or "Why can't you?" The anger rises in her. Though the anger is the eruption—the behavior they see—it is tinged with sadness. The sadness she doesn't know how, or where, to place.

This part of me learned from a young age that she was too much. She didn't know what to do with her feelings because those around her didn't know what to do with her feelings. I let her know it's okay to feel anything *that she is feeling. That her anger is not scary or wrong—it's normal. That her rage does not make her a bad child—nor does how she react in response to this rage. It is an outward expression of the confusion happening inside of her, caused by the "too much" happening outside of her.*

I ask her what she'd like to be doing if she wasn't burdened with the too muchness. "Singing and dancing," she replies. I let her know that I'll sit quietly while she does. I take delight in watching her dirty blonde hair bounce as she moves, her feet tapping in no defined rhythm. She feels my delight and moves closer to me—taking me in as safe now. I ask her what she is needing from me. "Just to be here with me," she replies. "You are not alone," I let her know. "I didn't realize it was you before. Now that I know, I will come to you when I feel you with me, and I will stay with you."

I let her know that I will check in with her often. We find a comfortable place for her to stay until I can be with her next. She chooses her room, with bright pink walls adorned with pictures she drew and some that she tore out of magazines. She lays down in her twin-sized bed, falling asleep. I gently tuck her in, letting her know I'll return soon.

As the name suggests, exiles are the parts that are buried deep within us. These are the fragile and vulnerable parts that our managers and firefighters are trying to protect from pain (or that they are trying to protect from reexperiencing pain once again). These parts have been touched most deeply by trauma or distress. It can feel like some exiles live in a space of limbo—believing the trauma is continuously playing out. In these cases, we might respond to the current situation as if the initial trauma is happening in the present. Have you ever gone home to your parents' house for the holidays and noticed that you started acting like a teenager again? That you started reenacting unhealthy ways of relating and behaving? This may represent an exiled teenage part of yourself that became activated and responded to old family patterns.

Although exiles often represent the younger parts of ourselves, they are not limited to our inner children or teenagers. While some exiles may be very young, others can represent a person's age when traumatic events occurred. For example, I have a 22-year-old exile that often arises beneath my protectors. She is not a child, but she is still a part of me that needs tender love and care.

Despite the fact that exiles can represent more than childhood parts, the idea of doing "inner child work" has come to the forefront of pop psychology in the past decade (many thanks to social media). Unfortunately, pop psychology versions of inner child work often force a connection to the inner child while ignoring the protective parts that are working hard to protect it. Just as you wouldn't force your own child to build a relationship with a stranger, you must first get to know your exiles—offering them safety and building a relationship with them—rather than bypassing protectors to do so.

Another difference between parts work and pop psychology versions of trauma treatment is that IFS emphasizes the importance of accessing Self-energy rather than the "adult self." We know that the term *adult* does not equal safe or regulated. We see this in the way that our own parts interact with others. Sometimes, our firefighters and managers behave in a way that doesn't feel safe, and our exiled parts may be confused by this. But when we come from a place of Self-energy, rather than from an "adult" part, we are able to offer our exiles clarity and pure loving energy. It can pour from us like a well. The Self becomes the ideal adult. This doesn't mean that other protective parts won't show up and enter into the system; it means that the Self is there to guide the parts and offer protection to the exile when they do.

♡ Reflection

What awakens for you as we begin to touch into exiles? How does the word *exile* sit in your system? How does it differ from the idea of the inner child? Does one phrasing feel better than the other? What happens as you acknowledge that there are multiple exiles within you, rather than one inner child?

EXERCISE

Delighting in an Exile

Think of an exiled part you'd like to get to know better, perhaps a young part of you. Imagine what this young part of you looked like at the time. What was this young one wearing? What did it enjoy doing? What excited it? Engage in an activity that this exile used to enjoy, checking in with this part as you engage. Maybe that looks like drawing or painting without judgment, searching for insects, swinging, walking barefoot, sprinting, or doing another enjoyable activity.

Following the activity, offer the young one your loving presence. Check in with it and notice how it felt during the activity. Locate any pleasant sensation in your body, offering the young one gratitude for the qualities it holds and offers within your system. Let the young one know what you admire about it and how proud you are of the activity you engaged in.

How is this young one taking in this delight? Is it able to hold it? Is there a safe place for this part to rest until the next time you can check in? Let this part know that you are there when it needs you, as you tuck it in for a nap, leave it to engage in another favorite activity, or leave it to quietly rest. Make a plan to continue checking in with this young one and delight in it in the future.

CONNECTING WITH EXILES

As we connect with our exiles, we often find they hold pieces of our own story that are missing or fragmented. We witness the depth of emotion our exiles hold, sometimes putting words to what we couldn't at the time. As we get to know these exiled parts, we can offer what they might not have received at the time of their trauma or distress. By offering Self-energy, or a sense of regulation and centeredness, we can move them through their burdens and offer them the safety they may not be familiar receiving. This was my own experience as I worked to unburden the 22-year-old exile that was becoming activated in the context of my marriage.

At the beginning of my relationship with my now husband, Brandon, I experienced a series of traumas—one thing arriving after the other. The common factor in those traumas was him, though they were not his fault. I was misled on a faulty job interview that quickly turned into sexual harassment, and I held so much blame for Brandon for not showing up for me during that time when I felt so isolated. Not long after, we got into a fight and I ended up getting robbed at knifepoint upon returning home—again, I put so much of the blame on him for not being with me when it happened. Following the birth of our first child, I experienced similar feelings of aloneness as I grappled with postpartum depression. The intensity of my depression was so strong that facets of it did register as trauma for me. I began to feel intense resentment toward Brandon during our daughter's first year. I pinned it on the fact that he did not help enough. I was doing it all, and I was feeling alone in the process.

We began to see a couples therapist trained in Intimacy from the Inside Out—a couples therapy model, developed by Toni Herbine-Blank, that is based on IFS. Like many partners who enter into couples therapy, our experience began with much shame and blame. I blamed him for not being there for me as I endured those traumas. I tried to make him see that this played out in our current relationship, which was exacerbated by parenthood.

During one session, our couples therapist, Deena, paused us as she noticed a part coming in for me.

"Would it be okay to work with this one?" she asked.

"Yes, I think she needs me to," I replied.

Deena checked in to ensure that Brandon was ready to bear witness to this part, to be present with me as I got in touch with her.

"Can you feel his presence and readiness to be with you and this part?" Deena asked.

I could feel it. His own Self-energy was coming through and being offered to me as I saw this 22-year-old part in distress on the couch in my old apartment. I felt her stuck there and was relieved we'd have Brandon's offering of Self-energy to rescue us. This part could finally receive from Brandon what it didn't receive at the time.

Eyes closed, I checked in with where the 22-year-old part was showing up in my body. I felt knots in my stomach. They weren't coming from another part—they were coming from her. She felt open but nervous being in Brandon's presence. She allowed me—the 32-year-old me—to sit with her on the couch she was laying on. Her hands were clasped around her stomach and her eyes closed. She was feeling sick for what she endured.

"It never should have happened," I told her.

"I should have known better," she responded.

"You couldn't have known," I told her, placing a hand on her shoulder. She allowed my hand to rest there.

I felt the safety being offered to me from Deena and Brandon. I allowed it to surround my heart, sending calming waves to the knots in my stomach. The 22-year-old felt the safety coming from me, allowing us to connect more deeply. I felt the despair keeping her stuck, like a magnetic pull to the blue velvet couch where she rested. I heard Deena's voice ask if this part knew we were safe now. She didn't. She felt like she was still too close to it, still in it.

Deena asked me to update this part on where we were now. I asked the part how old she thought I was. She wasn't sure if I was much older than her. I updated her that Brandon and I were married with a baby now. We moved from Los Angeles to Austin, and I was a therapist now, helping others who had experienced trauma, much like she did. She sat up and moved closer to me. The part of me that was yearning for something from Brandon, yearning for him to save us both, seemed to fade away. The 22-year-old part sunk into me.

"Well, this is annoying," I said as I opened my eyes, looking at Deena and Brandon. "It wasn't Brandon she needed all along. It was me."

Many of us have parts that hold on tightly to the idea of others saving us, like I had young ones that lusted after princes in Disney movies and managers that were waiting on a partner to fulfill missing needs of childhood. But it is both beautiful and devastating to find that our exiles are not waiting for someone else to save them. They are not waiting on someone else to change; they are waiting for us. We don't need to be much older, we don't need to have all the answers, and we don't need to be far along in our healing. We just need access to Self-energy. We just need to offer presence.

Along with the unburdening that occurs when an exile receives this sense of safety from Self-energy, there might also be grief or anger that arises. These feelings can show up for the parts of us who were waiting for so long on someone else, when we were there all along. They can show up for the exiles who didn't receive what they so desperately needed from caring others. These feelings can also show up at the prospect of having to be self-reliant once again. Regardless of the ways in which this grief, anger, or sadness shows up, we must make space for it all.

I went to couples therapy, like many, to change my partner. The most powerful moment I experienced was not my partner changing, but my connection with my own parts shifting. When I found the young exile that was waiting to connect with *me*, it allowed me to unburden the parts within me that were actually getting in the way of my connection with my partner. My feminist parts still cringe at the idea that I was waiting for so long for him to save me when, all along, my exiles were waiting for me to save myself, and I did.

♡ Reflection

What arises as you consider the idea of rescuing your own parts? Do you hold any fears or hesitation about being the one to save those young ones? If you feel unequipped, what feels as though it is getting in the way? Is there another part holding resistance to you being with these young ones?

EXERCISE

Connecting Exiles with Self-Energy

Turn your attention inside and think about an exile you'd like to connect with. Perhaps it is a younger version of you, or another part that feels like it touches close to the trauma. If you are not aware of specific exiles you'd like to get to know, imagine yourself at an age younger than you are now. How old are you? Imagine what you enjoyed wearing at that time. Imagine an activity you enjoyed doing. In order to further connect, simply observe yourself doing this activity. Perhaps offering delight to this young part of you if you're able.

Notice what happens in your body as you connect with this part of you. Notice whether any sensations arise. What texture or temperature is this exile? Does it feel comfortable or uncomfortable? Begin to notice what this part looks like, or what image it offers to you. How do you feel toward this one?

If you are experiencing any feelings other than openness or curiosity, notice if a protective part is coming in, holding fears around you working with this one. Let that part know that you are just gently getting to know this exiled part, and ask if it is willing to step to the side. If the protective part still holds resistance or fears, allow it to voice them, and keep checking in with it until it feels safe to step to the side. If the protective part is willing to step to the side, and no additional parts have risen, continue connecting with this exile, offering how you feel toward it.

If your feelings toward the exile are comfortable or pleasant, notice how that connects with certain sensations in your body, and send that energy toward this young one. Are they able to take it in? Imagine that your Self-energy is like a well that fills within your heart—a well that has a bright light illuminating it. What color would this light be? Send this colorful light toward the exile, and notice whether it is able to take it in.

How does this part feel toward you? If it feels comfortable or secure, see if it can imagine a comfortable and secure place where it would like to reside. This place can be imaginary or real. In this place, your exile can access anything it needs to build a sense of safety or security. If this part would like you to have access to this place, it can let you know how to find it.

Is there anything else this exile wants you to know as you part ways for today? How would this part like you to leave it? Alone but still in connection? Perhaps it would like to be tucked in for rest, left with a pet or stuffed animal, or playing a favorite game. Offer gratitude for this one coming forward today and for allowing you to connect.

EXERCISE

Nesting Dolls

Nesting dolls are wooden dolls that stack within each other. When you open the center of each doll, there is another smaller doll inside, until you get to the smallest one. Often, our parts are like nesting dolls in that they, too, are interconnected, with one leading to another. For example, we have some parts that we put on display to the outside world and some deeper exiled parts that may lay hidden, even to ourselves. Use these outlines, or design your own nesting dolls, to represent the interconnected parts within you. Begin with the largest outline, and draw a visualization of the part that is most visible to the outside world, and then connect to each part that lies deeper until you get to the smallest doll—the exile hidden inside. How do you visualize each part? What do they each represent? What burdens does each part carry?

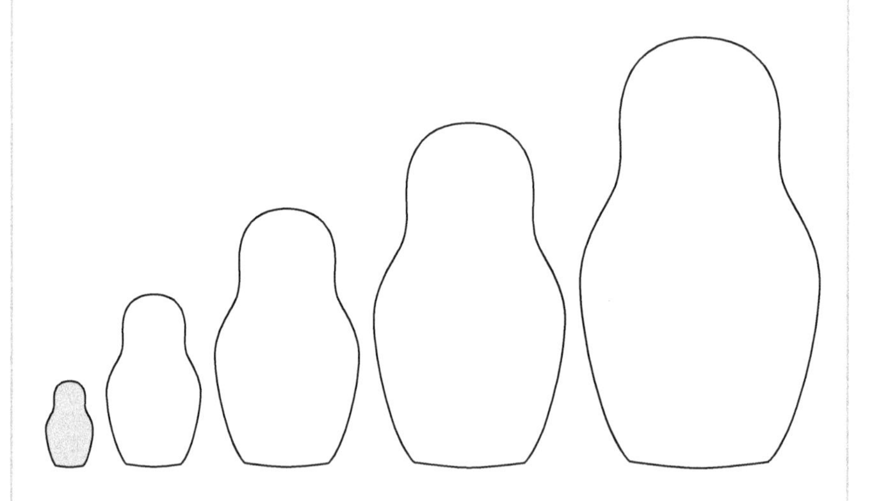

6

Accessing Self-Energy

I feel an illuminating in my chest and a clear line of energy down the center of my body. My face feels calm and my brain alert. I can feel the breath flowing through me, awakening my presence. I feel myself ready to connect to those outside of me. With my own parts at bay, present but settled, I am able to acknowledge them when they show up, sending the compassion they need to step to the side so I can be in full presence once again. In this state, I am able to be fully present with others—welcoming their parts without my own coming in to react or protect. I can view others in their full humanity and acknowledge my own. My body is at rest. I feel the flow of safety within me and can offer it to others. There is a peacefulness radiating within me. There is strength and trust in the connection my feet have to the earth and the bookend of my head looking up to the sky. I am safe. I am open. I am free. I embody safety. I embody openness. I embody freedom.

Although we all possess Self-energy, some of us have more access to it than others. In interpersonal neurobiology terms, the concept of Self-energy equates to the experience of being regulated (Siegel, 2012). In polyvagal terms, it equates to the experience of being in a ventral vagal state (Dana, 2018). It might also equate to the experience of mindfulness, in which we have the ability to watch our own thoughts without immediately reacting to them.

As discussed in previous chapters, IFS considers Self-energy to be a well of calming presence within. When we are in Self-energy, it doesn't mean that no parts are present, but that we can allow our parts to be present without becoming blended with them or allowing them to overtake the system. In Self-energy, we have compassionate access to our own internal world and can face it without judgment. It allows us to interact with our own internal world and others from a place of openness, as we hold acceptance and curiosity for each part that arises.

The experience of Self-energy is different for each person. When I experience Self-energy, I feel a distinct state within my body that exudes calming clarity. I can feel a soft energy flowing through me, connecting me with my own internal world and creating space to connect with the world outside of me. My breath flows gently without my needing to change or alter it. I feel alert but not alarmed. I feel centered, as though an energy creates a flowing line from my sternum to my head. There is openness flowing from my heart, as though a circle has formed around it. I am able to sit without judgment or agenda, while acknowledging any parts if they come forward. When I experience Self-energy, it is as though my body is saying "welcome" to myself and the world around me.

My own experience of acknowledging Self-energy transformed my work as a therapist. Although it was something I'd experienced prior to training in IFS, acknowledging and recognizing it in this new way allowed me to witness the stark contrast of *not* experiencing Self-energy. As a therapist, I care deeply for people. This deep caring often activates parts of me that are not so helpful in the therapy room—though they're trying to be. The parts most often triggered are my imposter syndrome part, who enters to tell me that I don't know what I'm doing, and my therapist part, who wants to offer tools and supplies to my clients.

At the core of each of these parts is the desire to be a "good therapist," as they care deeply about helping those with whom I work. But they don't recognize that in this bid to help, they get in the way of allowing me to be helpful to my full extent. For instance, when the imposter syndrome part is online, it lets in self-doubt, which blocks me from being fully open and aware of what is happening for the client sitting across from me. My parts distort how I perceive and interact with this *other* person's parts.

However, when I can allow Self-energy to flow toward these parts—briefly checking in with them, allowing them to feel the compassion and safety offered by this energy, and asking them to step to the side—I can return to center, where I am led by the Self rather than my parts. It reopens the space between myself and my client so I can have full awareness of and openness to their internal experience rather than getting stuck in my own. In the therapy room, Self-energy becomes a marker of presence. Can I be with this person fully? Can I make space and return to the Self when I can't?

EXERCISE

Tuning into Self-Energy

I invite you to close your eyes for a moment, turning your attention toward your breath. Allow it to flow naturally in and out without trying to change it in any way, just observing it and bringing awareness to it. As you breathe, notice if any sensations arise in your body, welcoming in any pleasant sensations and moving through any that bring you discomfort.

Now turn your attention toward your heart. Acknowledge and thank this organ for doing the difficult job of keeping you alive. Of pumping in rhythm, allowing energy to flow through your entire body. Imagine that your heart is emanating energy. Perhaps that energy forms in a circle around it. Imagine that energy flowing through your center, planting your feet firmly in the ground and your head toward the sky. Focus in on that energy—noticing its texture and noticing if there is a color or sensation associated with it.

As you stay with this energy, notice if any other thoughts or uncomfortable sensations enter in. If so, just notice them without asking them to leave. Each time you notice a part coming in, acknowledge it, lend it compassion from the center of your heart, and ask it to step to the side, returning to the energy at your center. Continue to do this until you can be strictly with the energy at your center, or until you come to a good stopping place. Thank the parts that came forward, and once again return to that center energy, acknowledging the strength of your Self-energy. Know that it will be there for you to return to when you're ready.

EXERCISE

Self-Energy Well

Turning inward toward your center, imagine that you are tapping into your well of Self-energy. This is a well of energy that offers you the 8 C's: calm, clarity, connectedness, curiosity, creativity, courage, confidence, and compassion. Imagine that you can feel this well beginning from your center and spreading this energy throughout your body.

Using your non-dominant hand and whatever colorful art tools are available to you, allow this well of energy to show up in front you in the blank space provided or on a separate sheet of paper. Allow it to appear from your heart and the movement of your hand rather than from your head.

EXERCISE

Connecting with the Self

Imagine yourself as a blank slate. Imagine that no parts are present because none had to form as adaptations in response to trauma. Imagine that instead of parts, all you have access to is the Self-energy within. Utilizing any art or writing tools you desire, allow this Self to be expressed through drawing or writing in the space below or on a separate sheet of paper. What might this Self look like? What might it feel like?

♡ Reflection

What was it like to connect with Self-energy? If you imagined it as an energy well, how big or small is the well? Does it have capacity to grow? What body sensations give cues to your own Self-energy? What might you need to build your capacity?

If you found it difficult to access Self-energy in the previous exercises, it is not because you're "doing it wrong." In fact, it's quite the opposite. It is likely you have some strong protectors working to keep you safe. This does not mean that you are at a deficit in any way. It means that you need more time to strengthen your Self-energy. If we consider how parts form in the first place—to help us cope with the tribulations we have endured in our lives—it makes sense that those of us who have endured more trauma or distress may have greater struggle in accessing this energy. Like any facet of our mental health, Self-energy is something we must work to strengthen.

When I am with clients in the therapy room, I aid them in strengthening their capacity for Self-energy by offering my own energy and acknowledging when I see theirs coming through. Each time I can acknowledge their Self-energy coming through, their nervous system can learn to remember that state of being. By getting to know what it feels like to be in this Self-led state, they can learn to return to this energy like an anchor, even in the most distressing of times. You, too, can aid your protective parts in building trust with the Self, slowly orienting to the safety of not having to come on so strongly. You can both acknowledge the important work of these protectors while lightly touching into the Self.

EXERCISE

Accessing Self-Energy

Consider a part who often takes over. A part who feels as though it becomes all of you when it shows up. Perhaps this is an anxious or depressed part. Perhaps it is one who takes over in an extreme physical way, causing your heart rate to speed up or your breathing to shift. When a part comes on strong, or you become blended with it, you can help it soften by accessing Self-energy. As you acknowledge the part who often takes over, ask the following questions to get to know it better and offer it Self-energy. You can answer these questions in meditation or by writing in a journal.

- How do you feel toward this part?
- How does this part feel toward you?
- Can it feel your presence?
- What are you noticing in your body? Is the sensation coming from you or a part?
- How would this part like to connect with you?
- Can it feel your loving presence? If not, what is getting in the way?
- If you could imagine an energy well connecting your Self to this part, what might that look like?
- Can the part feel this energy?
- Will the part allow you to turn toward it?
- How is it to be with this part?
- How close will it allow you to be?
- What is it needing from you?
- Can it take in gratitude from you?

EXERCISE

Parts Poetry

Tuning into your system and allowing judgment to step to the side, tune in to a part that has awakened within your system. Allow a word or phrase to come to mind that feels representative of this part. This word or phrase will be the title of your poem. Allow 10 or so words to join this one as the body of the poem. Continue to do this with other parts who arise as needed.

SELF-LIKE PARTS

As you are building connection with Self-energy, you may also find that you have Self-like parts who show up. It may feel as though you are experiencing the Self, when in reality it is a Self-like part in disguise. These parts often feel helpful, and their job often feels *so* important, but they don't allow us the same expansiveness we experience with the Self.

Most often, it is our managers who show up as Self-like parts. They are parts who seem to be aiding in our day-to-day life. Sometimes, it feels as though we would not be able to function *without* these parts. They fuel us with productivity when we need to be productive and pause us with rest when we need to pause. These parts seem Self-like because they help us succeed. They help us show up and get the job done. In contrast to the behaviors of some firefighters, which can be frowned upon, many of the behaviors of Self-like parts are actually rewarded within society.

So how do we know these are parts and not coming from the Self? When we are functioning from a Self-like part, we have minimal access to Self-energy. The drive and intention of the part is more powerful than all else. We lose the ability to take in outside information that conflicts with, or gets in the way of, the drive of this part. Our drive is toward meeting the needs of the part and carrying out the job it believes it's doing.

In my own experience, my therapist part often comes across as a Self-like part. While it holds much knowledge and intention in how to be a "good therapist," it doesn't allow me to be fully present. It attempts to be helpful by offering clients tools, interventions, and knowledge, but it does so because it wants to know that it is doing good work and getting it right. To an outsider, and even to a client, it may look as though I'm offering information that I've been trained to offer. But when this offering is coming from my therapist part rather than the Self, there is an agenda rather than a presence behind it.

In contrast, when I am working from Self-energy, the interventions I offer come from an embodied place of presence between myself and the client, in which I can tune into what their nervous system needs and gently offer invitations to access those needs. In my years as a therapist, this embodied presence has been my greatest asset. My ability to see the human in front of me, to take in and accept all the parts of them, is what helps me build a strong therapeutic relationship.

EXERCISE

Differentiating the Self from Self-Like Parts

I invite you to think of a recent scenario where a part who you know to be helpful showed up. Perhaps it is a part who helps you function in everyday life. Maybe it is a part who helps you work, gives you energy, or slows you down when needed. Think of the qualities of this part and the ways that it is helpful. How does it assist you in functioning? How does it aid in your survival? Let it know you acknowledge these qualities.

As you focus your attention on this part, what do you notice in your body? What is the temperature of the sensation—warm or cool? What is the texture—sharp or smooth? Focus on the body sensation as you continue to acknowledge these positive qualities within the part. Send gratitude toward this one, thanking it for aiding in your functioning. As you send it gratitude, can it feel you with it? How do you feel toward it? Let it know.

If the part is accepting of your gratitude and how you feel toward it, see if it might be okay to turn toward this part. Imagine funneling gratitude toward this part from your heart center. Notice if these feelings are coming from Self-energy. Do you feel relaxed and calm as you offer it these feelings? Do they feel genuine and present? Do you and the part have access to safety? If so, you likely have the Self online.

Notice how this Self-energy feels different from the energy of the part. As you focus on how this part feels different from the Self, notice where Self-energy shows up in or around your body. Can you feel that energy separate from the part? Where is the part showing up versus the Self? How do they feel different within you?

Then thank the part for coming forward and allowing you to offer it Self-energy. As you close this exercise, continue to allow your Self-energy to flow through, carrying it with you throughout the rest of your day.

Ultimately, Self-energy is the well from which we draw to regulate. For some of us, this well is deep and plentiful. We can tap into the abundance of energy that never seems to run out. For others, the well may seem out of reach, and we may not be sure where it lies or how to tap into it. Still, for others, the well may be present, though shallow. Our access to this well was formed from the energy poured in from those around us. If our caregivers were lacking in Self-energy, we may not have learned to tap into our own wells. If we had to form more and more parts in response to this lack of Self-energy from those around us, it may feel as though we have access to only a shallow or distant well. But I am here to tell you, the depth is not lacking. There is room for expansion. For each time you even dip a toe in to that well, or take a step closer to it, you are strengthening your capacity to be with and expand the Self. And you and your parts are so deserving of this expansion.

7

Body Sensations as Parts

There is a part of me that begins as an ache in the center of my spine. I feel the discomfort and try shifting my body to allow it to dissipate. It doesn't. I feel it grow, and it seems to expand like a ball. I feel intrigued by this part and allow the curiosity to flow toward it. I begin to feel an ache in the center of my shoulder blades, separate from the ball in my spine. The ball seems to shrink as I send curiosity toward it while this new ache expands. I ask the ache between my shoulder blades if it's willing to soften so I can get to know the ball. The sensation grows stronger—a signal it isn't willing to step to the side. I focus on the ache in my shoulders, checking in on what it wants me to know. The sensation shifts as I turn more attention there, the ache turning to a slight buzzing. A gray and blurry image comes to mind.

I ask the part what might happen if it wasn't there to do its job. I feel a sadness arise in my chest as the part responds, "You wouldn't be able to carry the weight." I take a deep breath, the part easing as I do. I let it know I understand why it's there. "I do carry a lot of weight," I acknowledge. It eases further. I ask how long it's been around, and it shows an image of me as a new mother, holding my daughter in my arms. It is indeed the beautiful weight I carry. It does feel like the I'm carrying the weight of the world in order to build hers. I check back in with the sensation between my shoulders, and it feels like less of a pain now. It has settled to a slight buzzing. I thank that part for coming forward and let it know I will check in with it and make space to further acknowledge it the next time it shows up.

Parts are intrinsically connected to the body. I've mentioned earlier that my own parts often introduce themselves as body sensations, like my head feeling heavy or a tightness within my chest. But our body sensations can do more than help us connect to parts and take us deeper in our exploration—we can connect to sensations *as* parts as well. We know that we hold memories, especially traumatic memories, not just in the brain but in the body. When we get curious about a particular sensation, we can explore facets of implicit memory and access material we don't have conscious awareness of.

This process is analogous to what happens when we experience an emotion. For most of us, we know we are experiencing a particular emotion because of how it makes us *feel*. Sadness may be linked to a sinking feeling in the chest, anger may be linked to a tightness in the stomach, and anxiety may be linked to a rapid heart rate. Therefore, we can deepen our self-knowledge and facilitate healing by deepening our connection with the body. *Not* including the body in healing practice can also have consequences. When we don't release emotions, stress, or traumatic memories held in the body, it can lead to chronic pain, immune deficiencies, and other physical ailments (Maté, 2003).

Given that trauma is held in the body, sensory stimuli can easily ignite a trauma memory when we're exposed to certain images, sounds, textures, scents, and even tastes that remind us of the past. For example, because of my past trauma, I have a startle response when I am alone and see my husband in my peripheral vision, even if I mentally *know* it is my husband and I am safe with him. Sometimes I catch myself saying, "Oh, it's Brandon," and still, my hands go up in a reflex, my body braces, and I let out a small shout. This is especially true when he comes up to my driver's side window when I am pulling out of the driveway. When my children are in the car, I am often talking to them or listening to JoJo Siwa, which immediately cues my parts that I am not 22, living in Echo Park. This grounds me in the present.

However, when I am alone, that bracing part of me comes up for protection, believing I am unsafe as I was at age 22, being robbed at knifepoint. I feel the bracing sensation within my body and my nervous system reacts with the freeze response before I can even register my husband's face. The nervous system can also react this way when vicarious trauma gets embedded in the body on a visceral level in response to events that we have heard about but haven't necessarily experienced. Feminist writer Jessica Valenti (2007) speaks about the precautions women take, such as holding their keys between their fingers when walking alone at night. This too can show up as a nervous system response, something women do without conscious awareness.

Although we may think that body sensations are only a window to uncomfortable emotions or trauma, they can also be an opening to pleasant memories and pleasure. In his body-based model of trauma treatment, known as somatic experiencing, Peter

Levine (2015) speaks about titration and pendulation, which involve moving back and forth between pleasant and unpleasant sensations. With pendulation, we oscillate our attention between the source of our pain and a grounding source of comfort. For example, we might focus our attention on the memory of a past trauma and then shift back to the here and now by noticing the sensations of our feet planted firmly on the floor. The key is to do this at a slow and gentle pace—titrating the physical experience—which gradually builds our capacity to deal with the more unpleasant sensations.

Although we often feel more drawn to explore sensations that present some kind of discomfort, *all* of our body sensations have the ability to help us gain further insight to our parts. We also build our capacity to tolerate the pleasant. As trauma survivors, our bodies often dim our physical sensations, which is another survival response intended to minimize physical or emotional pain. We can build our capacity to experience the pleasant by softly touching into body sensation as parts.

♡ Reflection

Notice what arises for you as you as you consider touching into your body. Does your body feel welcoming? Or do you hold fears about touching into your body? Perhaps those fears represent parts. If so, what are those parts afraid might happen if you connect with your body? Is there anything they need from you in order to ease?

EXERCISE

Connecting with a Pleasant Sensation as a Part

Allow yourself to settle into a comfortable position, inviting your body to relax as much as it is able. Then bring your attention to your breath, just noticing without trying to change it in any way. As you continue breathing, begin to turn your attention to a physical sensation in your body, perhaps beginning with just the rise and fall of your chest as you breathe. Noticing the cool air moving in and out.

Now bring to mind a recent moment of delight you experienced. Perhaps it is something as simple as spending time outside and feeling your face in the sun and feet in the grass. Or perhaps it is something more exciting, such as seeing live music and experiencing a moment of connection with the people around you as you sing a favorite song. Whatever it is, acknowledge that moment of delight in as much detail as possible.

As you bring this memory to mind, notice what happens in your body. Perhaps you feel a warmth or tingling in your chest. Perhaps you feel a bubbling in your stomach. Perhaps you feel a calming wave through your center. As you begin tuning into this pleasant sensation, you may notice some unpleasant sensations arise. This does not mean you're doing anything wrong; it may be another part coming forward. Should anything unpleasant arise, ask that part to dim as much as it's able to so you can check back in with the sensation you're focusing on.

Then continue to notice and connect with this pleasant sensation that arises within you, offering it some curiosity if you're able. As you offer it curiosity, imagine your heart opening to this sensation. Can it feel that energy coming from you? Is it willing to let you get to know it? How do you feel toward this sensation or part? Is there anything this sensation or part wants you to know? Does it feel that you're fully open to it, or can it sense some hesitancy? How long has this part been present? As you offer it curiosity, does it shift in any way? Is there an image, color, or texture that goes with it? Thank this one for coming forward, and then slowly bring your attention back to your breath, perhaps allowing this part to linger if it feels good to do so.

♡ Reflection

What was it like to tune into a pleasant sensation? Did it feel easy or difficult to stay with this sensation? If it was hard, did it feel like there was another part present that needed more from you? Is the pleasant sensation connected to a part who you can continue to access in the future, especially to help you move out of distress during unpleasant times?

EMBODIMENT AND THE WINDOW OF TOLERANCE

In pop psychology versions of trauma treatment, being embodied is seen as ideal, in which we work to develop a connection with the body. However, embodiment is not ideal when the body has experienced a lack of safety in the past. When the body has been harmed in some way, our protective parts work hard to disconnect us from it. Often, dissociative parts step in to take us out of our body and minimize physical or emotional pain. That is why tuning into the body is easier said than done. We can't push past these protectors in an attempt to achieve embodiment. Instead, we can gently move to an embodied space by working *with* protectors, even noticing how they show up in the body if we're able.

The concept of the window of tolerance is helpful in thinking about our protectors and embodiment within IFS. This concept, which was developed by Daniel Siegel (2012), describes the "optimal" zone of nervous system arousal in which we are able to function most effectively. When we are within our window of tolerance, our nervous system feels safe and secure. We are able to face our internal and external worlds, even when problems arise, with calm and clarity. We still experience stressors and other negative events, but we are able to handle them without becoming overwhelmed. However, when we are outside our window of tolerance, we move into a state of either hypoarousal or hyperarousal. In a state of hypoarousal, we may feel dissociated, tired, disconnected, or shut down. In a state of hyperarousal, we may feel anxious, overwhelmed, rageful, and impulsive.

Traumatic experiences can cause our window of tolerance to become smaller, making it much more likely we will move into a state of hypoarousal or hyperarousal in response to the daily stressors of life. When we do shift outside the window, our protectors come in to aid us in minimizing our distress or deactivating our exiles. The effects of hypoarousal and hyperarousal are our protectors in action. We may feel anxiety coming in with an escalating heart rate. We may feel dissociative parts stepping in to dim the physical or emotional pain. We may feel a rage burning in our core. Working with these protectors helps us move back inside our window of tolerance and, in turn, back toward Self-energy. It is here that we are safe to have the full experience of embodiment. We can feel Self-energy flowing through and can tolerate some discomfort, whether it stems from an unpleasant sensation or a part who is uncomfortable to get to know. We can then gently connect with the sensations arising in connection with our protectors to get to a space of ease with being in the body once again.

EXERCISE

Connecting Somatically with a Part

If it feels okay to do so, I invite you to close your eyes and settle into a comfortable position. Notice where your feet are landing. Your feet are your connection to the earth. You can return to this source of grounding that your feet provide whenever you need to.

Notice, and perhaps glance at, the sky above. Even in its vastness, you know that you are held and contained with the earth and sky as bookends. Observe your head in relation to the sky. Notice that it holds one of your most important organs: the brain. Become aware of any sensations that arise as you focus your attention on your head. Welcome each sensation with curiosity, and send gratitude to your head for all that it holds.

Now I invite you to move through your body—continuing this process of noticing, welcoming, and sending gratitude to your neck, shoulders, arms, chest, stomach, pelvis, seat, thighs, knees, calves, and feet. Upon your return to your feet, notice once again their connection with the earth.

As you reflect on the scan of your body, was there a body part or sensation that felt especially strong? If not, was there something you felt curious about and would like to further explore? If the exercise felt difficult or awakened something in you that you are not quite ready to explore, send gratitude to your body parts and sensations for allowing your curiosity in today. Now is an okay place to stop. Slowly open your eyes and orient to your surroundings.

Should you like to continue, I invite you to turn your attention toward the body part or sensation you noticed earlier. Focus your attention completely on it and just notice. Where is the sensation arising? How is it showing up? Does it feel warm or cool? Does it feel sharp or smooth? Does it feel fluid or stuck?

As you notice the quality of this sensation, I invite you to check in with any information it holds. What does it want you to know? How do you feel toward it? If the sensation were to fade or stop all together, what is it afraid would happen? Is there an emotion attached to it? Can it feel you there with it? As you get to know it better, how do you feel toward it now? Send some compassion toward the sensation. Thank it for allowing you to get to know it today.

As you close this time with your body, check in with what it might need from you. Nourishment? Rest? Tenderness? Perhaps allow that word or phrase to stay with you as you open your eyes and reorient yourself to your surroundings.

EXERCISE

Building Protection

Think of a protector you'd like to get to know better. As you turn inward to welcome this protector, notice if it shows up within your body or outside of it. As you turn inward toward this part, allow it to appear on paper. Using art tools of your choice in the space below or on a separate sheet of paper, draw how this protector would like to reveal itself and what lays on the other side of it. Perhaps it shows up like a brick wall or fortress. Maybe it shows up like a dam or fence. Allow it to appear in the way it would like to protect.

EXILES AND THE BODY

For those of us who have experienced trauma, it is not uncommon to experience flashbacks, which can occur emotionally or somatically. Flashbacks are the experience of feeling as though the trauma is replaying out in the moment. Through an IFS lens, flashbacks reflect the activation of an exile, which was closest to the initial trauma and most intensely holds the associated body sensations (Schwartz & Sweezy, 2020). This is another reason why it is crucial to move slowly and gently toward embodiment in trauma work, and also why we need to be patient before meeting our exiles. When we plunge toward the depths of embodiment, we may be reawakening trauma or tuning into a body sensation in a way that is retraumatizing. When we move gently into this territory, we are able to contract with our parts rather than igniting parts of ourselves that we are not yet ready to embrace or who are not yet ready to be known.

Because exiles hold so much sensation, the deeper we go, the more we may experience somatically. Some of the sensations in our bodies may feel new and different. As long as it doesn't move us out of our window of tolerance, these sensations are okay to experience. Many times, these sensations reflect physiological activation that has become trapped in the body following a traumatic event. As mammals, after a distressing or threatening event has occurred, the body needs to complete a series of instinctual movements to release tension and orient back to safety. These mechanisms can include shaking, trembling, yelling, and more. However, when the body is stuck in a state of freeze at the time of the trauma, this physiological activation remains trapped long after the event is over (McConnell, 2020).

When we connect with our exiles during the unburdening process, the body can finally access and complete these series of movements. By tuning into these parts and getting to know them somatically, we can uncover underlying impulses toward movement and respond in a way that facilitates trauma resolution. For example, if we feel the impulse to run, we can stand up and run in place to repattern the sensation of being trapped. Or if we feel an impulse to put out our hands, we can hold them out to the side to reestablish a physical boundary with a perpetrator that comes to mind. Each of these responses to our impulses can aid us in moving toward completion of the trauma. If you feel like you've run a marathon after doing trauma work, this is why. It is not just the brain working hard to build new neural pathways, it is the body working hard to build repair.

Without the body's involvement, trauma healing is incomplete. Through embodiment, we repair the wounds held so deeply by our nervous system. IFS allows us to build upon each layer of healing at a slow and gentle pace. We don't push past protectors or push toward embodiment before we are ready—before the body is ready. Instead, we listen to our internal protectors and listen to the sensations that arise along with them. Those sensations move us forward in our healing when we listen, move forward with them, pause with them, and attend to the impulses they offer.

EXERCISE

Somatic Release

Begin by focusing on your breath, knowing you can return to it throughout the exercise. While breathing evenly and gently, I invite you to think about a memory where you felt trapped or stuck. As you think about that memory, bring to mind an image that represents the most significant part of this memory. The image can be a metaphor or an actual image from the memory. Become aware of any sensations that arise in your body as you bring this image to mind. Notice where the strongest sensation is located and focus your attention there. Does the sensation have a temperature? A texture? Is there another image that arises with it?

As you notice the qualities of this strongest sensation, consider this sensation as a part. What does this part need from you? Is there an urge it holds? Is there anything this part needs in order to release? Perhaps you feel an urge to run. Perhaps you feel the urge to create a boundary around you with your arms and hands. Perhaps there is an urge to push against something. Whatever the urge, allow your body to carry the urge through.

As you move through this urge, notice your breath and allow it to release. What is happening for this part now? Where is it showing up in your body? Is there anything more it needs from you? If it needs further release, continue to move through any that arise until the process feels complete. Once the process feels complete, allow your body and this part to orient back to safety if you're able. Notice what happens in your body as you do so. Do you feel a sense of peace or calm? If not, what might this part need in order for you to access it?

8

Attachment and IFS

There is a part of me who feels like an internal hug. She fills my whole body with warmth, as though squeezing from the inside out. When my tears come, I can hear her whisper, "It's okay for them to be here, just let them come." She feels like a stroke of the hair, a bowl of matzah ball soup when I'm sick, a comfort. When the young ones get stirred within me, I can feel her arms wrap around them, making space for each. She delights in me when I feel doubt coming in. When I need to, I imagine I'm hiding beneath her skirt, like Mother Ginger in The Nutcracker, *and I scurry out when I feel safe once again. Her presence feels almost like a spirit, though it flows from the inside out.*

Sometimes, I nearly mistake her for Self-energy, but when I check in, she feels distinctly like a part. I feel her nurture, her care, her tending. Instead of energy coming from the heart, she offers that energy to my heart. When it feels as though I have a need that I can't access, she whispers sweet solutions, aiding in my need being met. I feel so much love toward her, and I can feel the love returned to me. She is the soft place for me to land, the reminder of "rest," the nurture I so desire. Sometimes she steps in to nurture those outside of me when it feels as though I can't access the nurture to offer myself. I know how hard she works, and yet I fear unburdening her, for I need this caring one within me—in all her grace and loving presence.

Our earliest internal experiences—those that will shape the system within—are formed by the people we rely on for care. It is these early experiences that become our attachment blueprint. They determine our outlook of the world and how we interact with others.

Although early attachment theories by John Bowlby and Mary Ainsworth suggested that attachment is a fixed state, recent researchers, such as Diane Poole Heller and Bonnie Badenoch, offer more flexibility in looking at attachment styles. Rather than viewing a person's attachment style as a life sentence, they view attachment patterns as more fluid and variable, in which we may even interact from different patterns depending on whom we are interacting with. This can provide a source of relief for those who believe they had a "good childhood" but struggle with relationships nonetheless. It leaves more room for repair in our attachment blueprints.

These more recent views also provide insight into how we can view attachment through an IFS lens. Namely, just as we acknowledge parts as adaptations, we can acknowledge attachment patterns as adaptations or parts. These attachment patterns—which help us map out how to best get our needs met in relational situations—can reflect one of four different types: secure, anxious/ambivalent, avoidant, or disorganized.

SECURE ATTACHMENT

Secure attachment, which correlates to Self-energy, is the ideal form of attachment in which we expect the world and people in it to be generally safe and secure. As babies, we develop this healthy attachment when our caregivers are responsive and attune to our needs most of the time. In toddlerhood, we use this newly formed secure attachment to wander away from our caregivers to play, knowing that safety is close by. For caregivers who are concerned whether they are meeting the needs of their babies enough to facilitate secure attachment, research indicates that these needs must be met correctly just 30 percent of the time (Tronick & Gianino, 1986). As we grow, and our caregivers continue to meet our needs while helping us build autonomy, we eventually internalize our safe caregivers so that even when they are absent, we can continue to access that safety within us through Self-energy.

Importantly, secure attachment does not necessitate that someone grow up with "perfect" parenting or a harmonious family life. In fact, we need conflict to build security. Through conflict, we learn to repair. The system comes apart and then reorganizes around the conflict to facilitate repair. Security requires responsive caregivers who tend to the needs of the child to the best of their ability, aiding them in making sense of the world by validating and putting words to the child's experience and exhibiting healthy rupture and repair. Better than a perfect caregiver is an imperfect caregiver who owns their mistakes (Tronick & Gold, 2020; Heller, 2019).

ANXIOUS/AMBIVALENT ATTACHMENT

Individuals can develop a blueprint toward anxious/ambivalent attachment if they grow up in an environment where their caregivers are unpredictable and inconsistent in responding to their needs. For example, their caregivers may be overly attentive and comforting at certain times, but absent or even intrusive at other times. In this environment, the caregiver may confuse what is happening within their own system for what is happening inside the child's system, which creates what is called misattunement. The caregiver may even interact with the child in a way that soothes the caregiver's own distress, creating more distress and a lack of connection for the child. For those of us who lean toward anxious/ambivalent attachment, there is often some significant access to Self-energy or Self-like parts, with protectors who come in to aid us in accessing connection (Tronick & Gold, 2020; Heller, 2019).

AVOIDANT ATTACHMENT

Avoidant attachment can develop when children are raised in an environment in which their caregivers are emotionally unavailable or even unresponsive to their needs. For children who experience this pattern of behavior, it might feel like their caregivers put up an emotional wall, blocking the child from internalizing the caregiver and the caregiver from internalizing the child. If the caregiver is cut off from their own internal world—and thus unable to connect with the child's world—the child is left to cope with emotions on their own. The child will internalize the pain of loneliness even though their caregiver was physically present, resulting in a smaller well of Self-energy from which they can draw upon. For those of us who live with this blueprint, we have often developed protectors to cut us off from our own emotions and the emotions of others. These protectors come in to lessen the intensity of those emotions and to lessen the pain of coping on our own (Tronick & Gold, 2020; Heller, 2019).

DISORGANIZED ATTACHMENT

Finally, those with a disorganized blueprint often experience a childhood in which their caregivers are a source of chaos or even terror. They are burdened with the plight of emotionally and physically relying on the very person who is the source of their fear—leading to an ever-present confusion of equating love with terror. Often, caregivers in these situations are externalizing the terror they hold within their own systems and are continuing a violent cycle of intergenerational trauma. Those of us who exhibit disorganized attachment often have a strong defense system developed to protect exiles from enduring further pain. This defense team is often a mix of firefighters and managers, some of which attempt to cope with the terror and others that have the urge or capacity to harm others. Because terror is often equated with love, and safety may not be known or internalized, when protective parts work hard to dim the pain, it may cause actual pain for the system (Tronick & Gold, 2020; Heller, 2019).

After reading about the different attachment styles, how does each land in your system? Do parts arise as you touch into how it might feel to experience each form of attachment? What do those parts want you to know about your own attachment experience? Do your parts feel resistant or welcoming as you tune into your own experience? If resistant, what fears do they hold?

PERPETRATOR PARTS

As the various attachment styles illustrate, our earliest caregivers leave the deepest imprints on the nervous system. As babies, we are learning to regulate, building our internal world, and viewing the external world through the lens of our caregiver. An infant's existence is quite literally validated by their caregiver. When that caregiver isn't present, an infant is not aware of their existence. In this sense, we rely on caregivers to aid us in developing a sense of self. When our caregivers offer chaos instead of calm, terror instead of safety, or confusion instead of clarity, parts step in to help us function, developing adaptations to meet our own needs and interact with an outside world that is perceived as unsafe.

In acknowledging how attachment lays a relational blueprint and how we develop parts to respond to the outside world based on attachment relationships, we must also acknowledge how we internalize those attachment relationships. Oftentimes, when our attachment styles were formed on the basis of unhealthy relational experiences, we internalize those relationships in the form of perpetrator parts, which are parts that seek to cause pain (both inwardly and outwardly) in an attempt to feel safe. When this pain is turned inward, this part can manifest as the voice of an inner critic who has internalized shame to avoid experiencing it from the outside world. In fact, there is a question we sometimes ask in IFS that gets at this notion of internalization: "Does this voice sound familiar to you?" We often find that the voice of this part sounds similar to a parent, a caregiver, or another person who caused us relational harm.

Other times, perpetrator parts can turn pain outward, leading us to perpetuate the cycle of trauma on others or reenact our own experience on others. As caregivers, this perpetrator part can emerge when we interact with our children in a way that we are not proud of. Just like a voice of a part, the behaviors of a certain part may remind us of one of our caregivers—especially those behaviors that caused us harm. It may be significantly less than what we endured from our own caregivers, but we are still flooded with shame when acknowledging the interaction.

When we feel perpetrator parts within, sometimes they can cause the same terror as the initial perpetrator, especially if they linger close to our exiles. Though they are similar to those who caused our exiles harm, they often exist as managers, trying to keep the exiles from enduring pain once again. Like any other part, when we get to know them, we can better understand why they showed up in the first place and work together to allow for unburdening.

EXERCISE

Getting to Know a Perpetrator Part

Bring to mind a perpetrator part who you'd like to get to know. Perhaps it is a part who speaks harshly to you. Perhaps it is a part who feels like it causes harm. Perhaps it is a part who resembles someone who has harmed you. As you bring this one to mind, notice if it feels present or distant. If it feels present, notice where it is showing up in or around your body. If it feels distant, notice what sensations arise in your body, whether or not they are connected to this part, as you bring this one to mind. Perhaps you'd like to keep it at a distance so it doesn't overtake the system.

Notice how you feel toward this part, and ask what information it is holding. What does this part fear would happen if it was relieved of its job? As you get to know this part, does it sound like anyone from your past? Tune in and see if you can find some familiarity in its voice. Once you do, ask this part if it is aware what its voice sounds like. How do you feel toward this part now, recognizing the familiarity of the voice? Let it know and see how it responds. If you feel anything other than openness and compassion toward this part, notice how the part reacts.

As you deepen your connection to this part, see if it can feel your presence with it. If so, is it willing to make more space for you? If this part represents someone who has harmed you, does it know? If not, update it on the harm that this person caused you and let it know where you are now. Let it know that the trauma has ended. How does it respond to this information? Is it able to soften?

When you're ready, thank this one for coming forward. Let it know you'll continue to connect to and get to know it, allowing it to soften. Then, if you're able to, send some compassion toward this part.

THE LOVING OTHER

In Matt Haig's (2020) beautiful work of fiction, *The Midnight Library*, Nora finds herself in an in-between space after she attempts to take her life. This in-between is her high school library, with her high school librarian inside, a woman who had shown her kindness when she most needed it. Nora's interactions with the librarian during her time in the in-between are a beautiful illustration of a loving other—the loving people or interactions we internalize who become soothing parts of our own system.

These loving others may be caregivers or parts of caregivers we've taken in. They may be teachers who were especially kind or took delight in us. They may be friends who showed up when it felt as though no one else was showing up. They may be therapists who supported us. They may be strangers who showed us kindness. They may be nurturing characters we took in from a TV show or movie. Even for those of us who did not have supportive caregivers, we can often think back to small moments with a loving adult in our lives, someone who looked at us with the delight we may not have received at home.

I think often of my fourth-grade teacher, Mrs. Sanchez. I thought of her often in my process of writing this book. When I was a child, she looked at me and delighted in me as if she knew that one day, I *would* be writing a book. She could find something special in each child she taught, but it always felt as though *I* was the most special. And although I was a smart child, there was something different about me and the way I learned. I would not find out until I was 34 that I was neurodivergent. Thankfully, Mrs. Sanchez was able to adapt to and encourage each child's learning style, including my own.

One spring, Mrs. Sanchez grew passionate about doing a unit on Dr. Seuss. We were all reading his books and noticing the deeper themes of sociopolitical commentary (explained, of course, in a friendly, fourth-grade manner). She'd decided we should create a play about his work. One day, I began reciting *Daisy-Head Mayzie*, a Dr. Seuss book (1995) that had become a favorite of mine. It tells the story of Mayzie, who was different from other children as a daisy bloomed out of her head. To my own surprise, I'd memorized nearly the whole thing. I will never forget the way Mrs. Sanchez looked at me as she told me that I should recite it for the play. I internalized that delight, that pride. I took it with me throughout my schooling, confused when other teachers *didn't* understand my way of learning and being.

Though I've grown up—and the last I heard of Mrs. Sanchez, she retired and moved into a sailboat in New York, as magical teachers do—I can feel that delight inside of me as if she is standing before me in this moment. She is a loving other within my system, there to tend to the young ones who worry about failure, who feel the shame bubble up each time I make a mistake, to calm the perfectionist who can't settle for anything less. She gives me the confidence of that nine-year-old child, standing on stage in her daisy headband in front of the whole school without worry.

While early relationships have some of the greatest impact, our attachment systems can also be altered in adulthood. The therapeutic relationship in particular offers one such opportunity for gentle attachment repair, in which the therapist becomes a loving other—offering safety, consistency, and healthy rupture and repair. Just as a toddler wanders away from their caregiver, checking back to make sure the caregiver is still watching and then returning to safety, the therapist offers a space to return to and drift from, allowing clients to build autonomy while knowing the therapist is still there.

While not a caregiver, the therapist offers an antidote to the attachment ruptures of our childhood by providing us with a disconfirming experience in the therapy room. A disconfirming experience is anything that is the opposite of what our system expects to occur (Ecker et al., 2012). For example, if we are used to being shamed after sharing our vulnerabilities, but we instead receive compassion and affirmation from the therapist in such moments, this is a disconfirming experience. Each time we experience this dissonance—the unexpected settling—it is new and different within our system, and it creates new neural networks in the brain. We can pause and allow the nervous system to adjust to this new way of being, allowing the loving presence to register within us.

These new and different ways of being also show our protectors—the parts of us that are prepared to be on the defensive against the vulnerable—that they don't have to work as hard. We can internalize what we receive from these loving others, fill our well of Self-energy, and form new parts within us that are there to offer tender compassion when Self-energy isn't available.

While some people already possess loving others within the system, those of us who haven't experienced many interactions of nurture or comfort can learn to internalize these loving others in other ways. Be it those we come into contact with, or an imagined one we can find within us. This can be especially helpful for those who haven't experienced many loving interactions yet want to offer nurture to their exiles. The loving other can aid in nurturing the exiles *and* offer containment for the adult.

♡ Reflection

What happens as you touch into the idea of the loving other? Can you feel your own loving other within? If so, what do you notice in your body as you bring this one to mind? What do they want you to know? What does their loving energy ignite within?

EXERCISE

Internalizing a Loving Other

Bring to mind a person you know, whether for a long time or a brief moment, who offered you comfort, security, and safety. This can be a person who is living or dead, and someone you know personally or at a distance. Imagine that person is sitting across from you, making those offerings. What might they say to you to bring you comfort, security, and safety? How might they interact with you to offer comfort, security, and safety? Write out their words and offerings in as much detail as possible in the space below or on a separate sheet of paper. When you are done writing, read it out loud, taking in the words. Notice what is awakened in your body as you take in the words of your internalized other.

9

Parts in the Driver's Seat: Dissociative Parts

There is a part of me who drifts away when danger feels too close. My head begins to lift like a balloon, and an exhaustion comes over me. Though my body is present, my mind is somewhere else. My eyes seem glassy and unable to focus on what is in front of them. As if I'm looking at the world without my glasses on. My connection with others drops from my system. Alone on my island, absent from my life. My body feels fuzzy, unable to touch into a singular sensation. This distance from my body feels somehow safer than being pulled into it. It is a relief that my mind has learned to make me disappear, though I fear being unable to disappear completely. As if I am asleep while awake, a goldfish floating with its eyes open, I numb to the pain the world tries to place on me.

We can't speak about parts work without speaking about dissociative identity disorder (DID). While IFS has normalized the idea that multiplicity exists within all of us, for some, this multiplicity exists with greater intensity. For some, trauma has caused existence as a system, meaning that rather than experiencing parts internally, parts of the DID system take the driver's seat and aid the host in interacting with the external world. For those with DID, parts, alters, people, and headmates (or whatever name feels most fitting) exist as a *dissociative* system. In this chapter, I will use parts language to refer to this system, but if you have lived experience with DID and that doesn't feel fitting for you, you can replace it with the word that fits best.

It is important to note that although I do have lived experience with dissociation, I don't have lived experience with DID. My perspective is that of a therapist who works with this population. In my experience, I have found that dissociation and DID are not spoken about enough in the trauma community, even though they are often comorbidities with PTSD and complex PTSD. I have also found that the old view of DID as "multiple personality disorder" still abounds, which is compounded by the sensationalism of DID that is portrayed within the media, such as Toni Collette's *The United States of Tara,* Brad Pitt's *Fight Club*, or James McAvoy's *Split*, among many others. I believe it is important for therapists to reframe and destigmatize DID and to gain knowledge in working with dissociative disorders, as they so often go overlooked and undiagnosed.

IFS provides one such framework for working with parts that can be very helpful for dissociative systems. It gives therapists new language for working with and conceptualizing DID. However, just because a therapist is trained in IFS does not mean they are equipped to work with DID, which requires specialized training. I also want to acknowledge that just because IFS uses parts language, it does not mean that it is appropriate for everyone with a DID diagnosis. For some individuals with DID, IFS can feel destigmatizing because it normalizes their own multiplicity. But for others, IFS can feel *more* stigmatizing and even like it encourages some of the facets of existing as a system. We can make space for the nuance. I hope this chapter is helpful for clinicians who hope to have a better understanding of how to support folks with DID, and for those who live with DID, to work with their own system from an IFS perspective.

MAKING SENSE OF DISSOCIATION

Early views of DID viewed dissociation as something that was pathological—as something wrong. Some psychologists even questioned whether it was a legitimate mental health diagnosis, believing it fell more toward a personality disorder because they believed those who exhibited dissociative symptoms were lying or exaggerating the truth for sympathy, which is a known symptom of some personality disorders. However, when we view dissociation from the trauma lens and consider the way IFS acknowledges multiplicity, or splitting, as a common attribute of trauma, it becomes easier to make sense of DID. Though uncomfortable, we can acknowledge the importance of dissociation in survival.

When we experience overwhelming feelings that are too intense for the brain to handle, our consciousness splits off, taking us out of the experience. We all dissociate to some extent. Small-scale dissociation can look like getting lost in a TV show or forgetting where you are going while driving. However, for those who have experienced trauma, dissociation is a threat response that splits us from consciousness so we don't have feel physical or emotional pain. Some people continue to experience conscious awareness when this dissociation is taking place, while others have a complete loss of consciousness. This can cause gaps in time and memory, as well as episodes of amnesia. For those who have endured repetitive trauma, such as sexual abuse, ongoing medical trauma, or cult or religious abuse, dissociation may become a common threat response.

♡ Reflection

How do you experience your own dissociative parts? Are you aware of how they show up for you? How do you feel toward these parts? How do you feel toward these parts when you reframe them as protectors? Are you aware of the ways these parts aid in your survival?

While dissociation aids in survival in the midst of trauma, and can protect us from being overwhelmed by traumatic material following trauma, those who experience DID begin to have dissociative episodes in their day-to-day lives. This can be extremely distressing, as these individuals may lose entire portions of time where they are unaware of their surroundings or actions. It also causes splitting to happen, in which the brain compartmentalizes parts, or ego states, that interact with the outside world while the consciousness is in a dissociative state (Haddock, 2001). These dissociative parts take on jobs or roles within the system, often coming online to interact in certain situations. From an IFS perspective, we often see the categories of managers, firefighters, and exiles within dissociative parts.

Acknowledging dissociation as an adaptation to trauma means we must heal the trauma to relieve the dissociative parts of their burdens. In the past, the treatment goal for DID was to integrate the system—to allow the parts to dissipate so they no longer needed to function as a system. As more trauma-informed research has come forward, some clinicians have shifted to a systems positive approach, in which the individual or system is allowed to determine the therapeutic goal. For some, this could mean integration. For others, this could involve strengthening the relationship with non-dissociative parts or gaining more control over the dissociation.

The antidote to dissociation is grounding. IFS has aspects of grounding and containment built into the model, but for those who experience DID, it is even more important to offer grounding that aids in strengthening Self-energy. That's because the experience of dissociation moves us away from the Self. When a dissociative part takes over, there may be little or no Self-energy available. Grounding somatically and with the environment can allow Self-energy to remain online so it can offer its centering presence to dissociative parts.

EXERCISE

Grounding Parts and Accessing the Self

Notice how it feels to plant your feet firmly onto the ground. Notice the sensation of your feet against the floor and the outline of each toe, perhaps allowing your toes to wiggle as you feel gravity connecting you. Now imagine that you have a well of electricity that moves from your feet to the top of your head, connecting you to the earth beneath and the sky above. As you connect with this energy, imagine it centers in your heart.

Continuing to check in with your feet against the floor, imagine that your heart is the center for this electricity, keeping you connected to your internal world and the external world at once. Should it feel as though the electricity dips or wanes, or you begin to lose connection with the ground, return to center. As you feel this connection with your internal and external world, offer this energy to the parts inside. Imagine a loving energy flowing through you, moved by the electricity, that extends forward to each part. Returning to center, allow this energy to dissipate, returning to where your feet are rooted. As you orient back to the world outside your body, perhaps notice one comforting object in your surrounding space for you to connect with.

TREATMENT CONSIDERATIONS

When we recognize dissociation within a client—whether DID or another on the spectrum—it's important to move gently into treatment. Because dissociative parts are sensitive to traumatic material, therapists should acknowledge the ways that some trauma modalities can worsen or intensify dissociation. For example, eye movement desensitization reprocessing (EMDR), a therapy modality that utilizes back-and-forth eye movement to reprocess stuck traumatic memories, can worsen dissociation, as can IFS or any other trauma modality.

Clients with DID may seem more well-versed in multiplicity and what it means to exist as a system, so a therapist may have the impulse to move more quickly into parts work. But instead, we must do the opposite, moving slowly and allowing *more* time to integrate grounding and containment work. That's because touching into traumatic material means touching into exiles. If protectors perceive that someone is moving too close to the pain of an exile, they become active. This means dissociative parts are likely to take the driver's seat to protect the system from touching in too closely to the exiles' pain.

When dissociative parts take over, exiles may also come closer to the surface, putting them at greater risk for hurt and pain and strengthening the roles of protectors even further. For example, a young exile who was hurt by their caregiver may find similarities within a romantic partner and take the driver's seat in order to repair the hurt caused by caregivers or to attempt a corrective experience. Should the romantic partner cause hurt or disappointment while this young one is in the driver's seat, it can cause further trauma that the exile may confuse with trauma from the past.

In utilizing IFS to treat DID, we strengthen the system by using Self-energy to access parts at a distance without allowing them to take over. We work with the "host," which is the main part or personality that controls the system most of the time, in order to access other parts without them taking over. Even if another part has taken the driver's seat, we can still access the host while the other part is online by accessing Self-energy. That's because the host holds access to Self-energy. In turn, we work to strengthen access to Self-energy when not in a dissociative state so we can access it more readily when needed.

It is important to stay consistent with all parts in offering them Self-energy or communication from the host. Though young exiles may require more tending to, when we give equal considerations to every aspect of the system, it offers more of a grounding presence and helps bring other parts into the present. This can look like using the same tone of voice with all parts (even if the communication is happening silently in your head), using similar language with all parts, and not giving anyone special treatment.

However, as established, dissociation is a survival response, so pulling someone out of a dissociative state can be a shock to the system. Even for folks who mildly dissociate, we don't want to move too quickly from a state of dissociation to a state of grounding. Instead, we learn to move gently out of this state by learning to access Self-energy and attuning to body cues that let us know we are moving toward a dissociative state. When we find the sweet spot just before the dissociation occurs—where the nervous system is beginning to sense threat, even though no threat is present—we can offer Self-energy to the dissociative part to allow it to relax and stay in the present. We can help it orient to safety.

For therapists in particular, one of the most important things we can do is stay consistent, and working with DID is no exception. Though dissociation may feel unfamiliar to many therapists, we don't work with systems because it is "fascinating." We are working with highly traumatized individuals who have developed survival mechanisms that have caused splitting. While we want to be system affirmative, we also want to offer consistent care to each part of the system. Though each part is not present during every therapy session, each part is taking in the session. Though a young exile may be present, we should treat it with the same nurturing energy we would offer an adult. Similarly, though an aggressive part may be present, we should treat it with the same nurturing energy we would treat a non-aggressive part. Our own consistency as therapist ensures that we are staying with and offering our own Self-energy, which is grounding for both us and our clients.

EXERCISE

Self-Led Meeting

I invite you to shift to a comfortable position. Notice where your feet are landing and where your head is positioned. Remember that you can always return your attention to your feet or head when you need. Before closing your eyes, notice one comforting object in your vicinity. If you're able to and it feels good, you can hold that object in your hands throughout this exercise, returning to it when you need. Identify the exits within the room and all other factors that point toward security. Then, if it feels okay, allow your eyes to gently close.

Notice the rise and fall of your breath, and see if you can stay with the same breathing rhythm even though you're bringing your attention there. If you have access, begin to notice how it feels to be in your body. If your body does not feel like a safe place to be in this moment, just notice the sensation of holding your grounding object or your feet on the ground. If it feels okay for you to be in your body, notice any pleasant sensations coming forward in this moment. If you feel numb toward your body, just allow it to be.

Then bring your attention toward your heart, noticing the energy within. If it is able to open, imagine your heart opening, sending warm energy to each part you'd like to get to know today. Imagine this energy is your life force, representing the Self. If you're able, send that energy toward your feet, planted firmly on the ground, and toward your head, held up firmly by your spine and shoulders. Allow this heart energy, led by the Self, to direct this meeting.

If it feels as though another part is coming on or taking over too strongly, move back toward the heart, offering that part the energy from your heart so it can settle. Allow your heart to guide you toward a secure, comforting place where you can hold a Self-led meeting with your parts. Perhaps this meeting is in the mountains under a tree canopy with stools made of tree stumps. Perhaps it is on the beach as you sit in the sand around a bonfire. Perhaps it is in your childhood bedroom, or a place of fantasy. Offer each part, alter, or headmate an invitation to the meeting—acknowledging it is okay if anyone doesn't feel comfortable being in attendance. Send each of them energy from the heart to allow them to come forward. Invite each part to take a seat, with the understanding they can stand or be in another position if needed. Who is present? Where are they positioned? Extend a goal for the meeting, allowing each part to accept or share their concerns. With the Self being in charge of directing the meeting, go around and allow each part to speak on their fears or to offer solutions or goals. If it feels good to you, you can journal about the thoughts of each part.

As each part comes forward, you can do a check-in by asking how you feel toward this part. Can the part feel this coming from you? If you feel anything other than curiosity, what might you need in order to offer curiosity toward this part? What hopes, fears, or concerns does this part hold? Are the other parts able to take in these hopes, fear, and concerns? Are you able to relay this to the others? What is this part afraid might happen should a solution be reached? Is there anything else it wants to share with you or the group?

Then thank this one for coming forward, offering it gratitude and compassion from the heart. Repeat this check-in with each part until they have all been heard. If parts cannot agree on a conclusion, set up a time to return to the meeting when you are ready.

When you are ready, slowly return your attention to the pleasant sensations in the body if you are able, or to your grounding object if that feels better. Allow the energy from your heart to flow to your feet and your head. Slowly orient back to the room, perhaps noticing different comforting objects. Give your parts time to settle and rest if needed.

WORKING WITH DISSOCIATION IN SESSION

Dissociative states are confusing and disorienting for those who experience them. The word *dissociation* is clinical, so many people don't have the language to describe what they are going through, and they may use other words to explain the experience. They may also not realize that not everyone experiences extreme dissociation. The Dissociative Experiences Scale (Carlson & Putnam, 1993) and the Multidimensional Inventory of Dissociation (Dell, 2006) are two helpful assessments for dissociation that can offer new wording around what is happening inside and clarity for treatment. In addition, be on the lookout for the following descriptions, which may indicate a diagnosis of DID.

Possible Descriptions of Dissociation

- Confusion
- As if I'm standing next to myself
- Voices inside my head
- Memory loss
- Zoning out
- As if someone is controlling me
- Cotton in my head
- Balloons in my head
- Feeling as though I'm not in the right body
- Disconnected
- Spaced out
- Like I'm not in my body
- In a trance
- Coming to
- Out of control
- Losing chunks of time
- Delay in feeling pain
- Things happening without my knowledge

As therapists in training, we are often taught that if we witness these signs of dissociation in session, we should put a stop to it. This says a lot more about the therapist's own parts experiencing discomfort with dissociation. When we can instead acknowledge it as a healthy mechanism of protection, we can appreciate why dissociative parts may need to come online during session. Therapy can be a vulnerable experience in which we access new ways of being that we haven't felt before. And while a therapist can offer safety, we cannot "create" or force safety on clients. For those who have never experienced safety, or who only experienced it before the trauma occurred, the offering of safety may not even *feel* safe. It also might not be a known concept, something they have *ever* felt. As long as we can offer clients grounding before the session ends, it is okay for dissociation to happen during session. In fact, allowing it to take place in the safety of our warm presence can allow this mechanism to complete its cycle, aiding the client in healing pieces of trauma and better controlling the dissociation.

As a presence on social media, I have gotten to know many folks who are seeking healing from DID, which has opened my eyes to the systems community. It is my hope that by using an IFS lens and recognizing the multiplicity within all of us, we are making more space for those who exist as multiples. If we can normalize multiplicity, we can also normalize dissociative multiplicity. In normalizing trauma, we can also normalize the effects of trauma, including DID. Dissociation is not something we never come across or don't come across often; it is merely something we have made folks feel as if they need to keep hidden. In IFS, we say, "All parts are welcome," and all facets and functions of those parts are also welcome.

10

Parts of the Therapist

There is a part of me who is a helper. She's there in the room with me when I'm with my clients. She shows up when I'm at home too. She worries if I'm enough for the people that come to my therapy room, seeking help. Sometimes she wonders if they would do better with someone more skilled. She shows up when my clients are in distress by offering books and tools. She is a fixer. She deeply believes she needs to know it all and deeply knows she's not supposed to. Sometimes this helper reminds herself, "As a therapist, you're not supposed to know it all" but she doesn't believe it—it's something she's read but hasn't internalized herself.

When my clients are in distress, this helper part activates other parts: the not-enough parts, the people-pleaser parts, the failure parts. The exiles who believe they were never meant to be good at anything. She lets me know I need to read more books and take more trainings. She lets me know that I need to be the best at what I do, that people are depending on me. I feel grateful exhaustion toward her. I can hold how hard she tries while feeling the weight of it. I let her know this. I let her know there is no best therapist. She feels confused.

"If there is no best therapist, why are we trying so hard?"

"For our clients," I respond.

"If there is no best therapist, how do we know if we're any good?" she asks.

"Our clients," I respond.

"But what if they're struggling?" she asks.

"Sometimes they will," I respond.

"So we worry," she says. "We learn more. We take trainings. We offer tools. We make safety plans."

"No," I say. "We keep showing up with our full presence, offering our open heart to each of them for 50 minutes a week, and trust they will be okay."

She settles, almost shrinking. I ask if she would be willing to hang out on the bookcase during my next session. She agrees but lets me know she'll pop back in if a worksheet is relevant.

"It won't be," I let her know.

She relaxes back.

Before I came to practice IFS, it felt like there was a cloud of anxiety lingering with me in the therapy room. A pressure would build in my throat as I sat with my clients. It felt as though I was constantly on the edge of offering psychoeducation, an intervention, or infinite wisdom. Our words are precious in the therapy room, and I wanted to choose the right ones. When people came to me in serious distress, I would attempt to offer whatever calming presence I could muster, but then I'd go right into crisis mode with them.

I distinctly remember driving home one day after offering what I could to a young client experiencing suicidal ideation. I was listening to Kacey Musgraves's "Rainbow" over and over again as tears streamed down my face. The lyrics reference holding tightly on to your umbrella during a storm, knowing that it will pass and that a rainbow is coming.

I couldn't stop thinking about this client and our session, hoping they would be able to see the rainbow ahead of them. At that time, I thought it was my job to create the rainbow. To close the umbrella, stop the rain, and paint each color in the sky. As I've grown as a therapist and gotten to know my own parts, I've learned that it's okay to be the only one who can see the rainbow. It isn't my job to force their eyes upon it, it's my job to hold it inside until they too can see it. Perhaps offering it in small doses, one color at a time, rather than a jarring spectacle that's too much to take in at once.

THE SELF OF THE THERAPIST

The first time I heard in my training, "Is that coming from a therapist part?" I laughed and said, "Of course not! That's the Self."

The group leader continued to check in with me until it was determined it was indeed a part. At first, the idea that we don't want to interact from parts in session, even therapist parts, didn't make sense to me. It felt like my therapist part held all the knowledge and interventions. It was my therapist part who knew what to do in crisis. It was her that got us through graduate school—a star student, no less. It was her that made sure when we weren't in session, we were constantly reading books on psychotherapy and taking trainings. It was her that was leading us straight to burnout. Now I'm not saying that we are supposed to leave all our knowledge and tools behind.

Rather, we can offer our knowledge and tools from Self-energy, or acknowledge when it is coming from a part, and check in with how it is landing for the person before us.

When I offer Self-energy in the therapy room, I feel centered and connected to the human before me and to my own humanness. I have infinite capacity for what my client brings to the session, rather than an agenda for where the session needs to go. I allow their system to dictate how we move rather than my own. I am connected in body and mind to the person before me, gently touching into what needs to be. I am aware of the relationship being built as I internalize the person before me and they internalize me. I am open and welcoming toward each part that arises. I feel the resonance between us, and somatic cues in my own body alert me to what might be happening in theirs. I am aware of what belongs to me and what belongs to them. When I feel parts arise, I am able to offer them a place to rest until the session concludes. If they need to be spoken for, I can offer this to the client: "I have a part who wants you to know…" or "I had a part come up who…" I have trust in the person before me. I have trust in myself. Our process will unfold in the way it needs for healing to take place.

The psychotherapy profession is a strange one. In many professions, there is a distinct training period that precedes going out into the field, but for therapists, we train in graduate school and continue to train throughout our careers. There is constantly new information to take in. In most professions, we get explicit feedback on our performance, while as therapists, we infer feedback based on client retention, our sense of how the session went, and our takeaways from supervision. We build ideals of what a therapist should be from the books we read, fellow therapist brains we pick, and trainings we take. In this, we can lose ourselves. We forget or don't believe that the most important part of the therapy process and the biggest predictor of healing is the therapeutic relationship. When we draw from our well of Self-energy and offer this to clients, rather than working from our therapist parts, we bring it back to the therapeutic relationship.

Many of us are drawn to this profession as wounded healers. This was no different from my own story. Having been a therapy client since I was 10 years old, those 50-minute sessions were some of my favorite parts of each week. It was a time to experience an adult delighting in me, listening to whatever I wanted to talk about, and reflecting myself back to me in a way I wasn't able to access myself. Often, we think we are the only ones in the therapy profession who come with our own wounded past but learn that this is not so as we grow closer with colleagues. We may also believe that we had to arrive at a certain place in our healing before becoming a therapist, but often the wisdom we take in for our clients we are taking in for ourselves as well.

IFS gives us permission to exist as a therapist with all our parts. We bring our history, our attachment wounds, and our current stressors. We bring the healing we have already worked toward and that we are yet to do. We bring our current knowledge, ways of being, and growth edges. Instead of being a "blank slate" from which clients can see themselves reflected back in us, we look at our clients with delighted eyes, allowing them to see their reflection through our eyes. Drawing from Self-energy, we don't abandon our parts, but put them to the side during session so we can tend to them at the appropriate time (yes, even the therapist parts, though they're a little sneakier).

♡ Reflection

What parts show up most often for you in the therapy room? These are the parts that hinder your Self-energy from coming through. What jobs or roles do these parts hold? What do they fear might happen if they didn't hold these jobs? What do these parts need to allow you more access to Self-energy?

EXERCISE

Parts of the Therapist

Imagine a client you're feeling stuck with. As you bring them to mind, think about how it feels to be in the room with them. What arises in your body as you imagine being in that room? Focus on that sensation, offering some curiosity if you're able. Is there an emotion that arises with the sensation? Is it old or new? Is it connected to a part within you? If so, notice if it's willing to come forward.

How do you feel toward this part? Let it know and see how it responds. How does it show up as you're with this client? What is it afraid might happen if it didn't show up? Notice what happens in your body now as you acknowledge this part's role. How long has this part been with you? How would it feel about not having to work as hard in session? What might it need in order to step to the side to allow you to fully be with this client?

Once again, imagine yourself in the therapy room. As you've gotten to know this part who arises, does it feel like you are better able to fully be with your client? If the part still feels present and blended, what else does it need from you? If you need to, go through this check-in once again until it feels as though this part is settled and you are able to offer your client your full presence.

WHEN PARTS SHOW UP IN SESSION

Our parts show up in session in different ways. Sometimes our parts see themselves reflected back from a client. Sometimes our exiles are stirred by a client with similar trauma. Sometimes a client reminds us of someone from our past and our parts respond to that history. Sometimes our parts struggle in being present with someone else's pain. Sometimes our managers jump in to resolve a crisis. Sometimes our parts get caught up in our own worth as a therapist and seek validation that we're doing our job well. Sometimes our parts have their eyes on the clock, feeling anxious about ending on time.

When my parts start coming in, I begin to lose my ease. I no longer feel my center or the breath flowing through me. My thoughts quicken. I begin to fidget more or watch the clock. As I feel the part trying to blend with me, I begin to lose presence with the person in front of me. Sometimes this means I miss what they've said or miss the meaning of what they've said. I move toward a space of agenda. The rhythm changes in the room. Sometimes it's subtle, but the person in front of me can feel the shift. We become a step out of synch in our attachment dance.

No matter our skill as therapists, parts *will* show up, even if we don't want them there. As we covered earlier, the goal is not to be free of parts, but to offer them our well of Self-energy so they feel heard and understood while knowing they don't have to work so hard. We can offer a reassuring "I've got this covered." While we don't have time in session to fully tend to a part in the way it may need, we can take a moment to acknowledge it and see if it's willing to hang out somewhere else until we can check in after session. We can also let the client know that a part of ours is showing up and needs some attention, taking a moment to be with it so we're able to return fully present to the client. This models the honoring of our own parts, just as we ask clients to honor theirs, and respects our clients by providing them with our best selves in the therapy room.

EXERCISE

In-Session Parts Check-In

Notice where this part is showing up in or around your body. Focus in on the sensation. Is it holding urgent information it wants you to know? If so, acknowledge the information it is holding and thank it for coming forward. Then draw your attention to the well of Self-energy in your heart center. Imagine that well is releasing a circle of light, offering loving energy to this part. Allow the part to take it in. Find a comfortable place in the room where the part can stay until the end of session. Let it know that you will find it there and tend to it in the ways it needs.

EXERCISE

Self-Energy Ritual

It can be helpful to build a ritual to tend to parts and access Self-energy before and after each session. Many therapists use meditation to settle into a day of sessions. Here is a list of other exercises that might work for you:

- Place a miniature in a sandtray after each client.
- Light a candle at the beginning of the day, blowing it out at the end.
- Do some parts journaling prior to your first session.
- Have an opening and closing song that feels settling for you.
- Notice and stay present with your body sensations.
- Tune into your breath.
- Offer your parts a spot to rest in different places around your office.
- Make a non-dominant hand drawing with a part.
- Have a grounding object nearby that a part is drawn toward.
- Check in with what your parts are needing and make a plan to meet those needs after your sessions.
- Find a settling word to offer each part that is present before beginning sessions.
- Spend time with your loving other.

BURNOUT PARTS

There are many ways to think about burnout. I draw from Emily and Amelia Nagoski's views (2019), who describe burnout as a physiological response where stress gets stored in the body and the stress response cycle is left incomplete. As therapists, especially those who work with trauma, we are particularly prone to burnout because we can't help but internalize our people and their stories. They, too, embed in our system, interacting with our parts.

When the stories and presence of our clients embed within, we have many parts who begin working overtime to care for us as protectors. Manager parts may work to protect our exiles from feeling pain that touches too closely to our own trauma. Firefighter parts might help us cope with the weight of doing a heavy and beautiful job. We might also have parts that believe we aren't allowed to struggle with our own mental health in the midst of being a helper. From an IFS perspective, burnout is a flood of too many parts working hard all at once without reprieve. When we don't spend time tending to these parts, they become active and are left continuing to do their job to their own detriment and the detriment of the system as a whole. The flavor of burnout as a therapist is different than what most people experience.

How does burnout show up for you? What are your early signals of burnout? What does it feel like within your body? Do you have any tools to contend with burnout when it arrives (or to prevent it from arriving)?

When I reflect on my own burnout experience, I think back to myself as an intern at my practicum site. My body was literally aching with burnout, yet I thought that was what I was supposed to experience. As I bring up that time, I remember my eyes were always drooping, I suffered from frequent headaches, and I experienced a constant pain at the base of my neck as if I was straining my head. My body was letting me know what was happening, but I wasn't listening.

At that time, I worked in a program where I had to drive long distances every day to see clients. I was constantly listening to audiobooks on my drive, as if I was cramming to be a good therapist before each session. However, when I think back to my proudest moments at that site, it wasn't when I was explaining polyvagal theory to clients, or even knowing what vagal state they were in. It was when I had enough capacity to play a Rihanna song to help a client ground themselves during a frightening dissociative episode. It was when I was able to sit with a teen who felt like they were an unbearable presence because of how intense their depression was at the time, yet I was able to exude that there was nowhere else I'd rather be than sitting with them in their depression.

Our parts hold a lot of beliefs about what we "should" be as a therapist because the world holds a lot of beliefs and expectations around being a therapist. Although many of these expectations come from media portrayals, I've never met a TV therapist who completely validated my own experience as a therapist. More often, I'm cringing at some portrayals of the therapy experience—unethical, unhelpful, or both.

From the isolation in keeping confidentiality to simply sitting in human presence for 50 minutes with 20 people a week, there is no job like this one. We reduce burnout by making space for *all* the parts that arise. By taking time to be with each of them and listening to their needs. By tending to them privately and allowing them to be seen by others in supervision or consultation when needed.

As my work with trauma has become more visible, I've taken on the beautiful work of consulting with therapists. In these consultations, we make space for the parts that arise in response to difficult cases. In these consultations, I have seen a universal thread, something I used to seek out as well. Therapists arrive looking for books, evidence-based practices, and concrete solutions. My therapist part has plenty of those to offer; she can look no further than the stack of books at my bedside, which rises from the floor because my nightstand doesn't have enough space. But when I explore further with therapists, pulling from my own well of Self-energy, what we so often find is our own parts getting in the way. That the stuckness is not inside our clients, but in our own parts. When they clear, we aren't left with a book, a perfect intervention, or evidence-based practice. We are left with ourselves.

11

Integration

There is a numbing part of me who once worked hard to keep me alive. It kept me at a distance from my pain by muting it. As I got to know this part, I learned that it held a lot of fears. It feared I would be overwhelmed by emotion if it let me feel. It feared uncomfortable emotions would last forever. It feared I would get stuck, unable to get out. As I got to know this part, I learned its intentions. While it was numbing me out, it believed it was keeping me safe. It believed it was keeping my pain from overwhelming me. It believed it was making it easier for me to live.

As I listened to its wisdom, acknowledging it as such, I began to make more space. I began to feel an opening within me. I began to move closer toward this part. I began to embrace it. Though I moved closer to it, the part seemed to make itself smaller. The numbing felt dim. It was able to be present while allowing emotions to come through, even those that were difficult to lean into. I asked this part how it felt about not having to do its job anymore. The first time I asked, it grew, making it known that I needed it to be there.

I continued to spend time with this part, getting to know it, offering it compassion, and allowing it to feel my presence. Eventually, when I asked how it felt about not having to do its job anymore, it responded that it was tired. It was ready to release its burdens. We built a sailboat together. Tenderly, with grief arising, this one who had been with me for so long was sent off to sea.

Integration is the coming together of your healing process. It is when the emotional healing, nervous system rebalancing, meaning-making, and trauma reprocessing align. This is an important part of the healing process and one we must give space to. It is a time when we are forming new neural networks and creating new pathways to build different patterns and ways of being. Because change is happening on a deep level within the brain and body, we must make space for integration—for registering this new and different way of being.

UNBURDENING

In IFS, integration can happen as parts ease and make new meaning or as they relax back from their jobs. The biggest way we see integration occur is in the unburdening process. You'll recall that exiles and other wounded parts carry burdens, which can stem from certain beliefs, family roles, the impact of trauma, and unprocessed emotions. In the unburdening process, the wounded part lets go of the burdens it has been carrying and allows them to be taken by one of the four elements: air, fire, water, or earth (Schwartz, 2021). To do this, we check in with the part and allow it to determine how it wants to release. Often, there is an impulse toward one of the four elements. We then imagine different ways the burden could be released. Perhaps it blows away with the wind, is ceremoniously lit on fire, is sent away on a boat, or buried in a special place. When working with a manager or firefighter part in particular—one who is being relieved of its job—the unburdening process can involve releasing that part completely from the system or allowing it to fade into the system where it is less likely to arise. The unburdening process can be ceremonious and powerful. It can also shake up a system that has carried these burdens for so long.

Sometimes parts are ready to unburden quickly while others can take years of working together before unburdening takes place. Though this book offers much Self-healing, I want to acknowledge that because this process can be so powerful, it may be best conducted with an IFS-trained therapist. In the neurobiological sense, unburdening literally creates new neural networks in the brain. While it offers relief, this can be a lot for the system to register and can even create discomfort at first. Our parts become familiar pieces of us, and when we register a new and different way of doing things, it creates a major shift in all aspects of our being, with Self-energy and other parts reorganizing around this shift.

Because we allow parts to guide us in healing within IFS, we don't unburden until a part is ready. Forcing a part to unburden creates further unrest within the system and may lead to a superficial unburdening or cause the part to come on stronger. As we connect with a part who may be ready for this process, we can ask, "Are you ready to let go of this burden?" or "Are you ready to let go of this job?" If the part responds that it is ready, we can begin the process. If it is not yet ready, we know there is more connection to do. Before we let a part go, we must truly connect with it, acknowledging how hard it has worked to aid us.

♡ Reflection

As you consider the idea of integration and unburdening, what happens within your system? Do your parts find comfort in this idea? Or do they feel resistant toward it? Notice what arises.

EXERCISE

A Check-In for Unburdening

If you have a part you have worked with extensively, one who has felt heard and seen, one whom you've noticed movement with, it may be ready to unburden from the system. This exercise offers questions to determine if this part is ready for the unburdening process. Move through each question in meditative or journal form, noticing what happens in your body with each question asked. Your body will be the biggest signal of this part's readiness to unburden.

- Where is this part showing up in your body?
- Is there an image that goes with the sensation?
- How has this part served you?
- How long has it been around?
- What job has it been trying to do for you?
- How does it feel about not having to do that job anymore?
- Does it hold any fears around letting go of this job?
- What burdens does it carry?
- How heavy do they feel?
- How does this part feel about letting go of those burdens?
- If it does not want to unburden, what else does it need from you in order to do so?
- If it is ready to unburden, how might it prefer to let go? Perhaps by sea, burial in the earth, drifting with the wind, or in a fire?

Following the unburdening process, we can expect to feel lighter. Interactions with our internal and external worlds shift. There may be small or large shifts in our functioning and capacity. There may be more ease for other parts within the system, which also shift their ways of being in response. As these shifts occur, we might also experience grief for the burden we've let go. This grief can arise from our realization that we held onto this part for so long or because that part is now missing. Other parts will organize around the absence of this one. The grief may feel like a deep sadness. Other emotions may intensify as well.

This doesn't mean the unburdening process was not helpful or didn't go right. It goes with the old trope: Sometimes it gets worse before it gets better. I often think of healing like a sling shot—we pull it back to launch forward. This can be true of the unburdening process as well due to its power. We must allow time to adjust to unburdening and, perhaps, to the absence of a part. We must give ourselves space to catch up to just how far we've come.

EXERCISE

Unburdening a Part

Bring a part to mind who may be ready to unburden, perhaps one you have worked with often. Imagine this part in its purest form, allowing an image to come to mind. Locate where it shows up in or around your body. With drawing materials, a separate sheet of paper, and any medium your hands feel drawn to, allow this part to manifest on the page. When your drawing feels complete, take in what you have drawn. What do you notice about how the part is showing up on the page? With the image in front of you, check in with what this part wants you to know. How do you feel toward this one? Let it know, and see if it can feel you with it.

If you can, offer it loving compassion and see if it is able to take this in. If so, begin to honor the ways this part has shown up for you. Let it know you are aware of how hard it has worked. Is it able to take this in? Check in with the burdens this one carries. What is it carrying in the job it upholds? How would it feel about not having to do this job anymore? How would it feel about letting go of those burdens? If it is ready, check in with how it might like to let those burdens go. With your drawing, you can hold a ceremony for the burdens of this part—letting it go by fire, air, water, or earth in the way that feels best for you and this part.

Following your unburdening, notice what you feel in your body. Do any pleasant sensations arise? Any unpleasant sensations? Do you feel lighter? Focus in on those pleasant sensations, imagining a place for the part and its burdens to rest—somewhere outside of your body. What emotions arise as you let go? Do they feel comfortable or uncomfortable? If they

are uncomfortable, can you offer the space to feel into them as your system registers this big step in your healing? When you're ready, return to your breath, orienting back to your surroundings.

ON HEALING

I used to think of "healed" as a destination people get to. That one day, we get to a place where our past is reconciled, our emotions don't overtake us, we are recovered from trauma, the nervous system is restored, patterns of distress we once fell into no longer happen, and we get a gold star as we graduate therapy. I thought that once we got to this healed place, distressing events became something we could bounce back from.

Now, as a therapy conductor and consumer, I can confidently say that I do not believe being fully healed is a thing. In fact, I wasn't fully healed when I became a therapist. Before you throw this book in the trash—please don't, you're almost at the end!—hear me out. Many of us arrive to healing work with the same view I once had. We sit down on the therapy couch and wonder, "How long is this going to take?" It's a valid question, as therapy costs time, energy, and money. There are many systemic factors that make it inaccessible. In considering that question, whether it shows up on the therapy couch or in your self-healing work, I also invite you to consider, "How long did it take you to get here?" Here to this book? To this place where you're ready to move deeper in your self-knowledge? To a place where healing and change don't feel as scary? To a place where you can acknowledge you need to make a change? To a place where the trauma feels like too much to continue living this way? There are no right or wrong answers for healing—just your own answers, whatever they may be.

As survivors of trauma, we often endure a lot of pain and distress prior to getting to a place where we seek reprieve. Parts of us minimize the extent of the trauma to minimize the distress, waiting for it to get "really bad" before we seek out healing. But when we have endured so much, the healing process is usually not quick. If trauma is the overwhelm of too much too soon, we must offer the antidote in healing work.

IFS allows us to slow down and be with all the parts that come forward. It gives us permission to be continuously healing. To let go of the finish line, knowing there will always be parts unfolding within us, and there is comfort in that. Our inner world is always responding to the outside world. There is comfort in knowing there is a system within us, ready to respond to whatever we endure from the world outside. That system is ready to adapt to each new circumstance, though we shouldn't have to endure the traumas that befall us.

In our healing work, we may be left with scars. We may be left with wounds that open for the first time or wounds that feel as though they close only to open once again. We may find pain we can't quite pinpoint or areas tender to the touch, though the bruise no longer shows. Though we may not come to a place of full healing, we can reach a place of continuous repair.

In a world that so often tells us to hide the parts of us that are too difficult to face, we can turn tenderly toward those parts, embracing them without fear. We can make space for each to be there and be with the grief of letting go when they are no longer needed. In making space for our own beautiful parts, offering the acceptance and compassion they deserve, we learn to offer that same compassion to parts of others. Your parts are welcome.

There are parts of me that feel easy to embrace. I know how hard they work to keep me alive. But they have not always been easy to be with. There were times I faced them with shame, having to look away rather than embrace them. There were times I wondered why those parts couldn't just stop. As I wondered, it felt as though they grew stronger. As if a hole was opening beneath me and sucking me in. Each time someone got too close to those parts, sometimes acknowledging them, I fell deeper into myself. Each part felt as though it consumed me, becoming all of me.

One day, it seemed I could see each part with new eyes. Meeting them for the first time. Fearful at first, I turned toward them, and as I did, they each began to relax back. As I met the depressed part, the heaviness faded. As I met the anxious part, the reckless fear turned to deep caring. As I met the people pleaser, she was able to turn inward instead of outside herself. As I met the 22-year-old, she acknowledged the depths of her trauma. As I met the suicidal part, she realized that she did not want to die but, instead, needed to find some relief. And as I met the numbing part, she allowed emotion to brighten within me.

As I stood with my parts before me, I was able to let go of the fear that once kept me from them. The fear that they would overtake me. The fear of judgement from others. The fear of letting them go. We stood in a circle, with compassion and openness flowing from my heart, and embraced. They didn't overtake me or show their cards to the outside world. They didn't come on stronger or drift too far away. I offered them compassion, and in return, they offered me the space to just be.

References

Badenoch, B. (2008). *Being a brain-wise therapist: A practical guide to interpersonal neurobiology*. W.W. Norton & Company.

Carlson, E. B., & Putnam, F. W. (1993). An update on the Dissociative Experiences Scale. *Dissociation: Progress in the Dissociative Disorders, 6*(1), 16–27.

Dana, D. (2018). *The polyvagal theory in therapy: Engaging the rhythm of regulation*. W. W. Norton & Company.

Daniels, G., Gervais, R., Merchant, S., Klein, H., Silverman, B., Lieberstein, P., Novak, B. J., Forrester, B., Kaling, M., Celotta, J., Sterling, D., & Kwapis, K. (Executive Producers). (2005–2013). *The Office* [TV series]. Reveille Productions, NBC Universal Television, 3 Arts Entertainment, Deedle-Dee Productions, Universal Media Studios, & Universal Television.

Dell, P. F. (2006). The Multidimensional Inventory of Dissociation (MID): A comprehensive measure of pathological dissociation. *Journal of Trauma & Dissociation, 7*(2), 77–106. http://www.doi.org/10.1300/J229v07n02_06

Docter, P. (Director). (2015). *Inside Out* [Film]. Pixar Animation Studios.

Dr. Seuss. (1995). *Daisy-head Mayzie*. Random House.

Ecker, B., Ticic, R., & Hulley, L. (2012). *Unlocking the emotional brain: Eliminating symptoms at their roots using memory reconsolidation*. Routledge.

Haddock, D. B. (2001). *The dissociative identity disorder sourcebook*. McGraw Hill.

Haig, M. (2020). *The midnight library*. Viking.

Heller, D. P. (2019). *The power of attachment: How to create deep and lasting intimate relationships*. Sounds True.

Levine, P. A. (2015). *Trauma and memory: Brain and body in a search for the living past: A practical guide for understanding and working with traumatic memory*. North Atlantic Books.

Maté, G. (2003). *When the body says no: The cost of hidden stress*. A. A. Knopf Canada.

McConnell, S. (2020). *Somatic internal family systems therapy: Awareness, breath, resonance, movement, and touch in practice.* North Atlantic Books.

Nagoski, E., & Nagoski, A. (2019*) Burnout: The secret to unlocking the stress cycle.* Random House.

Schwartz, R. C. (2021). *No bad parts: Healing trauma & restoring wholeness with the internal family systems model.* Sounds True.

Schwartz, R. C., & Sweezy, M. (2020). *Internal family systems therapy* (2nd ed.). Guilford Press.

Siegel, D. J. (2012). *The developing mind: How relationships and the brain interact to shape who we are.* Guilford Press.

Tronick, E. Z., & Gianino, A. (1986). Interactive mismatch and repair: Challenges to the coping infant. *Zero to Three, 6*(3), 1–6.

Tronick, E. Z., & Gold, C. M. (2020). *The power of discord: Why the ups and downs of relationships are the secret to building intimacy, resilience, and trust.* Hachette Book Group, Inc.

Valenti, J. (2007). *Full frontal feminism: A young woman's guide to why feminism matters.* Seal Press.

Walker, P. (2013) *Complex PTSD: From surviving to thriving: A guide and map for recovering from childhood trauma.* CreateSpace Publishing.

Milton Keynes UK
Ingram Content Group UK Ltd.
UKHW051351170923
428851UK00019B/282